# Limits to Competition

# Limits to Competition

The Group of Lisbon

The MIT Press
Cambridge, Massachusetts
London, England

© 1995 Massachusetts Institute of Technology, The Group of Lisbon, and the Gulbenkian Foundation

This book was set in Sabon by Publication Services, Inc. and was printed and bound in the United States of America.

Library of Congress Cataloging-in-Publication Data

Group of Lisbon.
  Limits to competition / The Group of Lisbon.
    p.  cm.
  Includes bibliographical references and index.
  ISBN 0-262-07164-9 (alk. paper)
    1. Competition, International. 2. International economic relations. I. Title.
HF1414.G77  1995
337–dc20                                     95-21461
                                                  CIP

# Contents

The Group of Lisbon    vii

Acknowledgments    ix

**Introduction: A Purposeful Planet**    xi
    A New Era of Competition    xi
    Problems of Contemporary Globalization    xiii

1   **The Making of a Global World**    1
    Images of the Global World    1
    The Finite Nature of the World    8
    The Emergence of a Global Civil Society    9
    The Reorganization of the World Economy and Society    14
    From National to Global Capitalism    21
    Capital Flows: The Primary Enzymes of Global Capitalism    23
    Made in the World    27
    Implications and Consequences    35
    The Crisis of Unemployment: The Major Social Issue of the Next Twenty Years    39

2   **The New Competitive Global World**    49
    Problems of Transition    49
    Features of the New Competitive Global World    62

3   **Can Competition Govern the Planet?**    77
    The Critical Choice    77
    Pax Triadica: Toward Global Governance    84
    The Predominant Answer: Competitiveness    89

4   Toward Effective Global Governance   107
    Cooperative Governance   107
    The Contract: More Than a Necessity—A Choice   109
    Words Are Not Enough: Global Cooperative Governance Implies Clear
    Operational Targets   111
    Growth of Noncompetitive Regimes   114
    The Next Step: Four Global Social Contracts   125

**Conclusion: Hegemony Will Not Work   141**
    Open Questions   141
    The Cooperative Pact   143

Notes   145
Index   159

# The Group of Lisbon

| | |
|---|---|
| João Caraça | Lisbon |
| Philippe de Woot | Brussels |
| Gianfranco Dioguardi | Milan |
| Louis Emmerij | Washington |
| Emilio Fontela | Madrid |
| Seiko Hirata | Tokyo |
| Pierre-Marc Johnson | Montreal |
| Claude Julien | Paris |
| Terry Karl | San Francisco |
| Daniel Latouche | Montreal |
| Robert McCormick-Adams | Washington |
| ✳ Riccardo Petrella | Brussels |
| Ken Prewitt | New York |
| Saskia Sassen | New York |
| Joel Serrão | Lisbon |
| Luc Tissot | Lausanne |
| Taizo Yakushiji | Tokyo |
| Hiroyuki Yoshikawa | Tokyo |
| Aristide Zolberg | New York |

# Acknowledgments

In the second half of the 1980s, the Calouste Gulbenkian Foundation sponsored what became the first phase of the project "Portugal 2000." In continuation of this fruitful initiative, the Foundation supported the activities and endeavors of the Group of Lisbon. The originator of the Group of Lisbon was Riccardo Petrella, head of the Forecasting and Assessment in Science and Technology (FAST) program of the Commission of the European Communities and professor at the Catholic University of Louvain.

This volume is the result of the activity conducted under the aegis of the group during 1992 and 1993. A collective work by nature, *Limits to Competition* would not have been possible, however, without the enthusiasm, determination, and capability of Riccardo Petrella, a fact that should be gratefully acknowledged here.

Many others should be thanked for their help; let us thank in particular Angelo Reati, from the Economic Affairs Directorate General of the Commission of the European Union; Jean-Benoît Zimmermann, professor at Marseille University; Henk Overbeek, professor at Amsterdam University; René Dreifuss, professor at Federal University in Rio de Janeiro; Lucio Ugo Businaro, from the Centro Studi Sistemi in Turin; Patrick Bellon, professor at Paris-Sud University; Paolo Logli, from the Development and Cooperation Directorate General of the Commission of the European Union; Mohamed L. Bouguerra, professor at Tunis University; Bruno Amoroso, professor at Roskilde University, Denmark; and Daniel Drache, professor at York University (Ontario), for their valuable comments and criticism on the first draft.

Special thanks are also due to Carl Tham, the general director of the Swedish International Development Authority; Hiroji Takeda, president of

Highman Rondo Cooperative Society; Michel Hervè, former member of the European Parliament; Robert Voorhamme, general secretary of the Flemish Trade Union Federation; Burkart Holzner, director of the University Center for International Studies at the University of Pittsburgh; and Harlan Cleveland, president of the World Academy of Art and Science, for having hosted the seminars and workshops between late 1993 and early 1994 that would result in this book.

Of course one cannot forget the considerable role played by Nadine Robberecht, Helene Henderson, and by Anne Dufour, who typed and corrected the various drafts of *Limits to Competition*. They have contributed to the long process of helping a committee of nineteen persons produce a coherent book.

Last but not least, it is a great honor to thank Dr. Mario Soares, president of the Republic of Portugal, who encouraged the group's work from its extablishment in 1992. His personal support of the aims and analyses of the group has been a great stimulus to the dynamism and commitment of all of its members.

# Introduction: A Purposeful Planet

This book is concerned with the role of competition in the process of economic and social globalization. It is devoted to the analysis of changes that are affecting the national economy, the growth of multinational firms, the role of the state, and the global environment. It deals with the new world configurations and examines the conditions and means for new forms of world governance.

*Limits to Competition* addresses the following questions: Can competition govern the planet? Is competition the best instrument for coping with increasingly severe environmental, demographic, economic, and social problems at the global level?

## A New Era of Competition

Competition (from "compete," which means "to seek together"[1]) is a powerful tool and an essential dimension of economic life among firms and countries. Competing for the efficient exploitation of natural resources and the generation of new means to satisfy individual and collective needs at lower costs and higher quality has contributed greatly to the improvement of both material and nonmaterial levels of well-being. As one of the driving forces behind technological innovation and productivity growth, competition has stimulated new levels of human aspiration and made great achievements possible.

Beyond economic life, competition is also one of the fundamental sources of mobilization and creativity in the political arena, cultural and artistic life, and sports. Democracy is based on both political competition (between groups and parties) and cooperation. It is about managing conflict so that winners are sometimes losers, and losers sometimes winners. It is based on fundamental agreements on the rules of the game that keep competitors from physically destroying each other, instead allowing them to resolve their conflicts through constant negotiation and renegotiation.[2]

With the growth of trade and industrial capitalism and under the influence of economic thinking, competition has been increasingly associated with the notion of a contest between rivals. In real economic life, competition has been equated with the act or process of defeating competitors. "To kill my competitors," was the answer a former director of Shell International's R&D division gave to the question, "Why do you invest in R&D?"

A new era of competition has emerged in the last twenty years, especially in connection with the globalization of economic processes. Competition no longer describes a mode of functioning of a particular market configuration (a competitive market) as distinct from oligopolistic and monopolistic markets. To be competitive has ceased to be a means to an end; competitiveness has acquired the status of a universal credo, an ideology.[3]

For capital (industrialists, bankers), competitiveness has become the primary short- and medium-term goal, whereas profitability remains the long-term goal and the raison d'être of the firm. For government departments of trade and industry as well as finance and employment, the competitiveness of the country is now the primary concern, with a view to attracting and retaining capital within its territory in order to secure a maximum level of employment, access for local capital to global technology, and the revenue needed to maintain a minimum of social peace.

Thus, for example, in Belgium the competitiveness of local firms and the structural competitiveness of the Belgian economy as a whole are the core concerns of the Central Economic Council, an influential multipartite organization that produces a report every six months on the degree of competitiveness of Belgian firms. A similar function is performed by the Competitiveness Policy Council in the United States (comprising industrialists, economists, and trade unionists), which submits an annual report to the president and Congress. The 1993 report is called *A Competitive Strategy for America*.[4]

The competition imperative among firms and among nations has also permeated and now directs the behavior of board members of universities and colleges, education ministries, trade unions, parliaments, the mass media, and urban planners.

## Problems of Contemporary Globalization

The globalization of finance, industry, consumer markets, information, and communication infrastructures and services—not to mention high-technology-based military security—has accentuated the transformation of competition from a means and a particular mode of economic functioning to an ideology and an aggressive goal for survival and hegemony.

Competing in the global economy—characterized today by the emergence of new competitors, especially from South and Southeast Asia—has become the everyday slogan of multinational corporation advertisers, business school managers, trendy economists, and political leaders. People are told that a new global economy is in the making, the main players being North American, Western European, and Japanese-based multinational corporations. Through localization and transplants of production facilities and fierce competition—or alternatively, via strong alliances to enable more successful competition at the world level—the global networks of multinational corporations are reshaping the sectoral and territorial configuration of the world economy, from the automobile industry to telecommunications, electronics to pharmaceuticals, textiles to civilian air transport. The new global economy looks like a battle among economic giants where no rest or compassion is allowed the fighters. The globalization of the economy seems an inexorable process enabling world networks of financial and industrial firms to amass an unparalleled power of decisionmaking and influence over the destiny of millions of people throughout the world.

The globalization of the economy is only one dimension, albeit the most important one, in the emerging reconfiguration of the world and the globalization of human affairs. A global wave of democratization is another major dimension. Strikingly enough, the surge in democratization dates to the early 1970s, the same priod that saw the beginning of the globalization of finance and capital markets. Starting in Southern Europe (first in Portugal, and then in Spain and Greece), it spread to Latin America, affected some Asian countries, and swept through Eastern Europe and the former Soviet Union. Even in Africa, often considered too poor to produce democracies, the end of apartheid in South Africa represents a major step in this process. Many factors, most of them country- or area-specific, explain the emergence and fast growth of the global wave of democratization. Diffusion, demonstration effect, and "contagion," are the descriptive terms most frequently mentioned by analysts. Within this dynamic context, two interrelated processes have played and still play an important role.

The first is "the development of formal non-governmental organizations and informal group networks devoted to the promotion of human rights, protection of minorities, monitoring of elections, provision of economic advice, and fostering of exchanges among academics and intellectuals, all interested to promote democratisation."[5] This movement has helped create the political space for democratization. Its efficiency has been enhanced by regional and international organizations that have been revitalized with the end of the cold war, which have adopted democratic promotion as a means of keeping the peace.

The second process is represented by the global development of information and communication systems and networks. With the spread of television and communications satellites in the 1970s and shortwave radios and fax machines in the 1980s, authoritarian governments have found it increasingly difficult to control the availability of information internally. Global communication networks not only demonstrate to people in one country that autocrats can be removed in another; they often show just how it can be done. The globalization of the communications media is in fact an old and well-known process. Forty years ago, people were beginning to talk of a "planetary village."[6] Today the "civilization of satellites" (as opposed to the "civilization of the soil"), the "world communication superhighway," and the "global information society" are just a few popular slogans and concepts that describe an epoch-making series of changes.[7]

It is difficult to say whether these changes will favor peaceful interaction among cultures and ultimately benefit the promotion of local and regional identities and the development of a new global civilization. They could, conversely, engender new forms of cultural domination at the global level based on nonmaterial goods and services—a form of domination more profound than that based on material goods produced by Coca-Cola or Sony.

Recent developments in information and communication technology have also contributed to the emergence of another significant phenomenon:

the rise of a global civil society. This phenomenon is linked to the new wave of democratization previously discussed as well as to the explosion of major social problems and challenges worldwide and the perception of their commonality among today's 5.6 billion people. Banal but typical examples of this perception are reflected in a global consciousness of living in a common "spaceship earth" and sharing "a common future."[8]

In addition to environmental problems, globalization is increasingly associated with demographic explosion, mass unemployment, mass immigration flows, growing organized crime (particularly the drug trade), insecurity linked to the proliferation of nuclear weapons, and ethnic and religious conflicts as well as new epidemics (such as AIDS) and the resurgence of once-defeated traditional epidemics (such as malaria). Above all, globalization is nourishing the fear of a clash between the strictly limited number of "haves" and the "have nots."

The gap is impressive between the powerful process of economic globalization at the level of finance and firms and the weakened capability of national public authorities to cope with the explosive nature of most social, economic, environmental, and political problems across countries and regions of the world. Despite the new wave of democratization, the absence of organized forms of socially accountable and democratic political governance at the global level emerges as the fundamental weakness of the present world configuration. This absence has two major consequences. First, it significantly reduces the ability of local, national, and regional forms of political governance to exert control over economic, social, and political events and processes—a fact that political leaders are increasingly admitting. Second, it makes it impossible to reconcile the interests and operations of economic globalization (led by competing forces seeking to maximize their profit and influence) and the interests and operations of the globalization of human affairs (as represented by the comparatively weak networks of nongovernmental and voluntary associations and goodwill from a minority of people in academia, labor, industry, and government).

Furthermore, new dangers characterize the present situation. Just when democratization is spreading, so are inequality, the destruction of the environment, the concentration of power, and the rise of nationalism. Most important, unmanaged competition strengthens these adverse tendencies just as democratization is beginning to create the conditions necessary (such as the rise of the global civil society and the growing consensus among international organizations) to do something about it. The result, especially in the traditional parliamentary democracies, is a fundamental crisis of legitimization of the state that is not balanced by an increase in legitimization of new forms of world governance based on liberalized and deregulated forces.

This book is an attempt to identify and recommend the many positive approaches that can be explored to overcome the present situation. In this respect, *Limits to Competition* does not take a stand against competition per se. But it does take a stand against the excesses of an ideology of competition that insists on excluding other ways of organizing economic, political, and social life. Competitiveness is not the only value that can operate in the service of individual countries of the world community. The competitive market is not everything. It cannot impose its logic on other human and social dimensions, especially when it pretends that it has to ignore them. Not every commodity is available on the competitive market. As a report from the Business Council for Sustainable Development has emphasized, "the traditional logic of business that ignores human and ecological aspects is unable to respond to present changes and population needs."[9] It is now increasingly acknowledged that so-called economic rationality cannot command—even though it claims the right to do so—other spheres of individual and collective life, such as education, family behavior, community development, and the functioning of democratic institutions.

There are structural limits to excessive competition, inasmuch as it does not address the major challenges of:

- socioeconomic inequalities within nations and among nations, and the marginalization of large parts of the world;
- the exploitation of, and damage to, global life-support systems (for example, growing desertification, soil erosion, extinction of animal and vegetable species, ocean and river pollution);
- the concentration of power in largely unaccountable economic units (multiterritorial or multinational firms, global information and communication networks).

Accordingly, *Limits to Competition* shows that the pursuit of competition in search of profit as the single legitimate overarching concern of firms is unjustified as the main motivation for private and public choices in a world of increasingly global processes, problems, and interdependence. Competition among firms alone cannot handle long-term world problems efficiently. The market cannot properly discount the future: it is naturally shortsighted. Putting together thousands of myopic organizations does not enable them, individually or collectively, to see the reality and acquire a sense of direction, or provide governance, order, and security. The same applies to competition among nations, which, in excess, inevitably leads to a rat-race mentality and global economic wars and hinders the ability of policymakers to address national and global priorities.

All in all, where the interests of competing firms are associated with the interests of competing nations, the results are tantamount to a counterintuitive evolution against market mechanisms, for example:

• the creation of new forms of protectionism or defensive industrial policies. To increase the ability to compete with other nations, the state helps its local firms by protecting them or giving them artificial advantages;
• technonationalism, by restricting the flow of knowledge as a possible competitive production factor for other nations;
• bilateralism, as a means to keep competitors out of the market.

In other words, market competition alone is self-defeating in a world of competing nations. The same applies to market competition in the context of competing regional blocs. It seems, therefore, that an efficient system of competitive markets requires a cooperative framework among nations at the global level, that is, socially accountable and politically democratic forms of global governance.

*Limits to Competition* argues that the response to present and immediate future needs and opportunities demands a system of cooperative governance. Only by linking the multitude of socioeconomic networks at various territorial levels around visible targets and common objectives can one realistically hope to achieve social justice, economic efficiency, environmental sustainability, and political democracy, as well as avoid the many possible sources (economic, religious, political, ethnic) of global implosion.

Societies today are confronted, mutatis mutandis, with the same problem as nineteenth- and early twentieth-century societies. The problem was excesses of capitalism. Nineteenth-century efforts leading to representative democracy and the improvement of the social conditions of workers as well as the history of the twentieth century have in fact tended to counterbalance these excesses. Thus:

- against the tendency of competitive capitalism to reduce competition (monopoly capitalism), antitrust laws were enacted;
- against the tendency to exploit labor, laws were enforced preventing child labor, regulating working conditions, and upholding minimum wages;
- against the tendency to exclude the poor, social welfare programs were set up;
- against the tendency to deceive, laws controlling advertising and regulations governing consumer protection were established;
- and, more recently, against the tendency to externalize environmental costs, regulations for environmental protection have also been enacted.

These achievements contributed to the gradual establishment of the national social contract that is the basis of the modern economic and social development of advanced Western societies. The state, as a promoter and guarantor of the public general interest, intervened. The excesses of national competitive capitalism were softened. This took place in a national framework, where the nation-state was able to influence the operations and evolution of national capitalism.

Today the source of the problem is the same; that is, globalizing competitive capitalism has its excesses, but the framework for its operations and the role of the key players, in particular the nation-state, have changed. Because of, inter alia, the erosion of national markets, the state is now an instrument that is weaker vis-à-vis the forces of globalization, whereas the networks of multinational corporations have been able to significantly increase their ability to exert influence and control. This creates a serious problem, because most of the excesses of competitive capitalism are reemerging on a global scale. For instance:

- in a context of market deregulation and liberalization, financial and industrial capital mobility at the world level is bypassing the regulatory framework based on the nation-state;
- in a growing number of financial and industrial sectors there is a strong tendency toward oligopolistic structures. Regional and global interfirm alliances and mergers are allowed on the basis of the argument that one has to favor a nation's or region's competitiveness at the global level;
- labor legislation and social welfare programs are being weakened or slowly dismantled while mass unemployment is becoming one of the major social issues of the next fifteen to twenty years. The enhancement of local firms' competitiveness is claimed to be the best way to re-create jobs;

- indifference to marginalized populations is again increasing;
- delays or cancellation of regulations concerning environmental protection are increasingly requested for the sake of competitiveness.[10]

The situation described above demands therefore a new type of global economic governance. The likelihood that a "global state" will be created to negotiate with "global industry" to soften the excesses of global competitive capitalism is rather slim, at least in the next twenty to thirty years. And to expect that global competitive capitalism will itself soften its own excesses is equally unrealistic. What then can be done?

In the view of the Group of Lisbon, a need exists to develop a new generation of social global contracts, both tacit and explicit, to identify the best cooperative solutions in the interests of the greatest number of people and nations. These global contracts should be seen not as static bureaucratic events but rather as elements of a multifaceted, evolutionary process. *Limits to Competition* identifies four priority global contracts. The "enzymes" for the development of cooperative governance are new modes of citizenship invented and experienced at urban, national, and global levels. Not surprisingly, however, these new modes are opposed by a variety of malevolent forces such as racism, social exclusion, ethnic conflicts, and religious wars.

The Group of Lisbon is comprised of nineteen members from Japan, Western Europe, and North America with different educational backgrounds and experience in business, government, international organizations, and academia. The group has received financial support from the Calouste Gulbenkian Foundation to meet in Lisbon, as well as from the Spanish-Japanese Nao Santa Maria Foundation, the Swiss Economic Tissot Foundation, the Fratelli Dioguardi Foundation in Italy, the Yoko Civilization Research Institute in Japan, and the Science and Technology Center and the National Institute of Scientific Research, both located in Quebec. The name of the group also has a symbolic meaning. Its activities began in 1992, the year of the five-hundredth anniversary of the so-called discovery of the new world. As is well known, Portugal was the mother country of the fifteenth-century era of *descobrimentos* (discoveries). By using the word "discovery" we do not wish to imply any specific historical meaning. That the deliberations and recommendations in support of a new global endeavor based on cooperation rather than conquest could come from a group of Europeans,

Japanese, and North Americans meeting in Lisbon, a city with such a heritage, was considered significant. Hence the name Group of Lisbon seemed fitting.

The group was created on the initiative of Riccardo Petrella, head of the FAST program at the Commission of the European Union in Brussels. He has been the principal drafter of *Limits to Competition*. The process of signing on the nineteen members was simple and effective, thanks in large measure to fax machines. Two full group meetings were convened in Lisbon and a few smaller editorial sessions were held in Nagai (Japan), Warnant (Belgium), Lisbon, and Montreal to provide each member the opportunity to actively contribute to the book's development. Transparency, motivation, and trustful cooperation were the three ingredients that allowed the group to work toward its common objective.

The Group of Lisbon is intentionally composed only of members from Japan, North America, and Western Europe. Representing the most developed and powerful countries of the world, the group seeks to address their responsibility and ability to cope with the rising tide of new global problems and prospects. These parts of the world have a great deal of experience in promoting and preserving cultural diversity, democratic institutions, human tolerance, and social accountability. They also share a vivid collective memory of the great human disasters that have occurred when their leaders and their populations have been guided by extreme nationalism, fundamentalism, and totalitarianism.

This does not mean that, in the opinion of the group, Japan, North America, and Western Europe should determine the agenda and simply present it to the rest of the world. Nor does it mean that the countries and peoples of the world do not have the ability to take action themselves, or that they should remain passive and simply be acted upon. What the group wants to stress is that the very powerful countries of Japan, North America, and Western Europe can no longer pursue their current policies.

A new sense of sharing a common history and destiny at the global level is emerging. The group believes that the world cannot be seen as an arena for hegemonic conquest. It is time to address the perverse consequences of excessive competition and to go beyond the short-term logic of self-survival. It is the profound conviction of the members of the Group of Lisbon that Japan, North America, and Western Europe must continue to develop their enormous potential in science and technology and use their economic wealth with a view toward designing and implementing—together with the other peoples and countries of the globe—a new global world that can reconcile economic efficiency, social justice, environmental sustainability, and political democracy, rather than continuing to serve exclusively their own utilitarian interests and their fight for global dominance.

The group believes that given the enormous surpluses of material and nonmaterial goods and services, massive scientific and technological potential, and high levels of education and experience among the millions of people throughout the world, it is now possible to establish such commitment. It is the primary responsibility of Japan, North America, and Western Europe to mobilize humankind's ingenuity to address as a priority the basic needs and aspirations of the world's population.

# 1

## The Making of a Global World

This chapter argues that the globalization of human affairs is no longer an abstract concept but a hard fact. The global world is the result of a profound reorganization of the economies and societies of what have hitherto been called the first world (the Western capitalist developed countries), the second world (the communist, state command economies), and the third world (the underdeveloped and poor countries of Latin America, Africa, and Asia). This division of the world no longer exists. Another type of configuration now characterizes the geo-economy of the planet, with the countries of Asia having developed into one of the new gravitational poles of the globalizing economy and society.

This global transformation is redefining the central role played until recently by the nation-state, national capitalism, and the wealth of nations, as well as by industrial modernization and the national social welfare contract. This chapter suggests that globalization is a process different from both internationalization and multinationalization. "Made in the world" is putting an end to the national economy and capitalism as the most pertinent and effective basis for the organization and management of the production and distribution of wealth.

### Images of the Global World

#### A Communications Village?
A first impression of the global dimension of today's human condition is derived from watching the evening news on television. In thirty minutes, a flow of images from every part of the world on every aspect of life transforms the viewer into a minuscule entity floating in a galaxy of worlds all belonging

simultaneously to the same history on the same planet. This is particularly true of people from the "triadic world," which is composed of the three richest regions of the world: North America, Western Europe, and Japan and the "minidragons" of Southeast Asia. To some extent it is also becoming true for an increasing number of people from China, India, Indonesia, Latin America, and Africa.

When watching the news on television, most of us are not aware that 80 percent of all images broadcast throughout the world are taken from just three major world image banks; but we do realize that we are viewing a world reality that is common to everybody. The twenty-four-hour information services provided by Cable News Network (CNN)—a private American network—via satellite is the much-cited example of the new era of global information.

Watching the CNN news is now part of the daily routine of those global travelers (managers, industrialists, bureaucrats, media people, and scientists) who make up the globalizing elite. It is seen in the same airports and hotel rooms where the global travelers find the other common ingredients of their daily environment—that is, newspapers (*International Herald Tribune, Financial Times, Wall Street Journal*), magazines (*Fortune, Time, Newsweek, Business Week, The Economist*), "global" food (that is, so-called international cuisine)—and where they can pay with global credit cards for long-distance calls increasingly made through the same global telephone networks of multinational firms.

The situation of ordinary men and women is fairly comparable. Their global daily routine includes watching the same films (the majority of which are American) on TV (the overwhelming majority of which are made by Japanese-owned networks of factories transplanted throughout the world) and listening to the same music produced and commercialized almost simultaneously in all countries without any major variation (other than market potential) among different peoples, cultures, or regions.

What we refer to here as "the Madonna economy" is actually a process that is unifying (essentially by homogenization) the consumption of information and communication goods according to the same (market) logic and in the same way (mass advertising via global infrastructures and networks) that the Coca-Cola world or the Levi's jeans universe used previously. It would be misleading, however, to conclude from this that there exists a "planetary village." There is a big difference between perceiving a situation in which people are gathered together in a world arena to watch the same performance (and not all people are invited!), and living the community experience of shared goals, means, and actions that the word village evokes. For example, in 1984 the *Missing Link*, a report by the International Tele-communication Union (ITU), set out the following objective: "By the early part of the next century, virtually the whole of humankind should be brought within easy reach of a telephone."[1] This objective was revised six years later because it was recognized as unrealistic: in 1990 "the area of Tokyo alone had more telephones than all of Africa, with its population of 500 million people, and Japan had more telephones than the developing countries of Asia, Africa and South America put together."[2]

Similarly, it would be an overstatement to say that our planet is already encircled by underwater, in-ground, and airborne digitized highways and superhighways of communication, as some advertising brochures from IBM, Alcatel, Siemens, Sony, Mitsubishi, BT, NTT, Ericcson, and others would like us to believe. We are still far from the world as a genuine global network. Nevertheless, international information and communication networks are growing rapidly.[3] A process of rewiring the world is taking place.[4] And the family of acronyms is expanding every year; a few examples of the intrafirm telecommunication networks that practically all large multinational business corporations have installed follow:

| | |
|---|---|
| TYMNET | The largest and most successful international producers' value-added network (VAN) for services |
| SWIFT | Society for Worldwide Interbank Financial Telecommunications |
| SITA | Société Internationale des Telecommunications Aéro-nautique, the largest closed user group network serving more than 300 airlines worldwide throughout some 170 countries |
| RETAIN | IBM's private network |
| GLOBECOM | Citybank network, interconnecting overseas branches in some 100 countries |
| SABRE | American Airlines Reservation Network and other computer reservations systems such as AMADEUS, GALILEO, WORLDSPAN, SYSTEMONE, ABACUS |

This phenomenon is still in its infancy and the potential for further developments is considerable, as is shown by the tremendous expansion during the last four years of the Internet, the popular online network (with more than 20 million users in 1993). Difficulties, however, will develop as much of the current technological euphoria will be cooled by the limits of technology itself, the inadequacy of the services supplied, diversity among countries, and the great variety of cultural contexts.[5]

### Mega-infrastructures for World Products and Services

Another picture of this global world in the making is offered by transport infrastructures. Each day 55,000 airplanes fly around the globe. In 1990 they accounted for 2.1 trillion passenger-kilometers, approximately half of which comprised scheduled international services. To make this level of service possible, we have been building larger airports, with huge parking lots and modern commercial centers employing more and more people (70,000 are employed at London's Heathrow airport). Air traffic is constantly being integrated by increasingly sophisticated computer monitoring and control systems; airplanes themselves are being transformed into flying terminals of a global computer system. A megamachine is growing. In many respects air transport is already both saturated and inadequate. In the next ten to fifteen years, the evolution of the air transportation global world will be rather turbulent; in the meantime, it is hoped that the adverse effects of airline deregulation will be eliminated.

The "pilots" of this megamachine are less the national public authorities (because of the wave of privatization, deregulation, and liberalization), and more the aircraft industry corporations, air carriers, travel agencies, tour operators, and, to a growing extent, the vendors of computer reservation systems (see table 1.1).

Another megamachine, namely automobile transportation, is helping to shape the new global world, possibly to a less visible degree than air transportation but not in a less influential manner. There are about 400 million automobiles on the planet today, and they are suffocating most large cities. They require more than 100,000 kilometers of highways and an even a greater number of national and local roads. They consume oil—3.6 billion barrels per year. To produce and distribute such a large quantity of oil every

**Table 1.1**
The "pilots" of the air transportation megamachine (1990–1991)

| The largest world groups in the aerospace industry | The largest world groups in civilian air transport | The largest travel agencies | The most important tour operators | The most important vendors of computer reservation systems |
|---|---|---|---|---|
| Boeing (USA) | American Airlines | American Express | Holland Int. | Sabre |
| United Technologies (USA) | Delta Airlines | Woodside | Jetset Tours Int. | Covia |
| British Aerospace (EC) | British Airways | Carlson | Thomson | Worldspan |
| McDonnell Douglas (USA) | Air France | Rosensluth | Wagons-lits | System One |
| Allied Signal (USA) | Lufthansa | Wagons-lits | Bennet | Galileo |
| General Dynamics (USA) | KLM | Business Travel Int. | LTU Group | Amadeus |
| Lockheed (USA) | Swiss Air | Hogg-Robinson | Wallace | Abacus |
| Textron (USA) | SAS | Halpag Lloyd | Arnold | |
| Deutsche Aerospace (EC) | United Airlines | Havas | | |
| | Jal | Thomas Cook | | |

Sources: Commission of the European Communities, *Panorama of EC Industry 1993*, Eurostat, Luxembourg, 1993; World Travel and Tourism Council, *Report 1991*, and *Travel Industry Yearbook 1991*.

day, a huge infrastructure (including insurance, legal, and health services) has been created and is constantly expanding.

It is easy therefore to understand why the Gulf War was waged and why many other similar wars will be fought in the future if public "pilots" and rules are further weakened, and the threat to the security of oil supplies and markets increases. For the time being the idea of a global car has failed commercially. However, the global transportation megamachine has grown stronger and more widespread. In addition to the buyers and users, the "drivers" of this megamachine are the automobile and components manufacturers and the oil companies (see table 1.2). Altogether they employed 15,123,207 people in 1991.[2]

The situation has not changed significantly within the oil company group during the last thirty years. However, major changes have reshaped the identity of the "drivers" among the car and components manufacturers. In 1964, Japanese firms were almost nonexistent, producing only 600,000 cars; whereas U.S. and European manufacturers combined to produce 15.4 million cars. In 1991, they increased production to 18.8 million units. Japan meanwhile produced 9.9 million cars—one-third more than the United States and one-fourth less than all European manufacturers combined.[7]

What is important to note—in addition to such industrial reshaping—is that the trend of the global car megamachine depends less on the hardware and infrastructure (such as cars, highways, gasoline) and more on the place that the car occupies in the value system of contemporary societies. Each of us is so culturally bound to, and dependent on, the global world represented by the global car megamachine that, if cars were to disappear, the consequences would be inestimable. This is why the proposition of cities without cars, though seemingly a good idea, sounds so revolutionary (and hence unrealistic) to nearly everybody. The same is true of the computer. We may live without nuclear energy (most people would like to), but it is impossible to imagine that our economy and society could function without the computer, and hence without electrical power.

Our growing dependence on cars and computers, for example, and the constraints this dependence brings have contributed to the development of another image of the global world—the finiteness of the system in which we live.

**Table 1.2**
The "drivers" of the global car megamachine (turnover in 1990, in million ECU)

| Oil companies | | | Car and components manufacturers | | |
|---|---|---|---|---|---|
| Royal Dutch Shell | EC | 83,034 | General Motors | USA | 96,640 |
| Exxon | USA | 82,720 | Ford Motor | USA | 76,551 |
| Mobil | USA | 46,299 | Toyota Motor | JPN | 53,778 |
| British Petroleum | EC | 46,172 | Daimler-Benz | EC | 41,570 |
| ENI | EC | 32,882 | FIAT | EC | 37,758 |
| Texaco | USA | 32,062 | Volkswagen | EC | 33,091 |
| Chevron | USA | 30,265 | Nissan Motor | JPN | 32,330 |
| Elf Aquitaine | EC | 25,325 | Renault | EC | 23,664 |
| Amoco | USA | 21,958 | Chrysler | USA | 23,359 |
| Total | EC | 18,537 | Honda Motor | JPN | 23,314 |
| Petroleos De Venezuela | VEN | 18,117 | Peugeot | EC | 23,088 |
| Pemex | MEX | 15,228 | Robert Bosch | EC | 15,507 |
| Atlantic Richfield | USA | 14,117 | Mitsubishi Motors | JPN | 15,164 |
| Nippon Oil | JPN | 13,497 | Mazda Motor | JPN | 14,712 |
| Petrobas | BRA | 12,219 | BMW | EC | 13,214 |
| Idemitsu Kosan | JPN | 11,272 | Volvo | EFTA | 11,034 |
| Repsol | EC | 10,922 | Isuzu Motors | JPN | 8,390 |
| Phillips Petroleum | USA | 19,664 | Nippondenso | JPN | 8,208 |
| USX-Marathon Group | USA | 10,413 | Suzuki Motor | JPN | 6,780 |
| Petrofina | EC | 10,229 | TRW | USA | 6,404 |
| Nestlé | EFTA | 9,589 | Audi | EC | 5,895 |
| SUN | USA | 9,260 | TOTAL | | 570,451 |
| Statoil | EFTA | 9,104 | | | |
| Showa Shell Sekiyu KK | JPN | 8,970 | | | |
| Unocal | USA | 8,345 | | | |
| Imperial Oil | CAN | 7,538 | | | |
| Ashland Oil | USA | 7,041 | | | |
| Nippon Mining Co | JPN | 6,534 | | | |
| RWE-DEA | EC | 6,049 | | | |
| Mitsubishi Oil | JPN | 6,029 | | | |
| TOTAL | | 624,391 | | | |

Source: *Panorama of EC Industry 1993.*

### The Finite Nature of the World

We have come to realize that we live in a finite world and that our immediate and long-term future depends on our ability to cope with the constraints this reality presents. Even before the first United Nations Conference on Population and Environment in Stockholm in 1972, and the publication in the same year of *The Limits to Growth*,[8] which popularized many of the concepts and analyses that had been treated in other reports and forums since the 1950s,[9] people had begun to realize that our planet's resources were not infinite. The work that has been undertaken since then, including the publication of the Brundtland Report *Our Common Future* in 1987,[10] which coined the now accepted term "sustainable development," has contributed to public acceptance of the finite nature of the world.

As a further result of the growing process of globalization of human affairs, it has become clear that the finite nature of the world is linked not only to the limits of the world's physical and natural resources but, more important, to the limits determined by human and social interdependence, complexity, and cohesion that interact with physical and natural limits.

The concepts of one earth and our common future have given our recent awareness of the finite nature of the world its full sense of direction. There also seems to be a growing acceptance of the principle of responsibility and accountability vis-à-vis humankind and future generations.[11] Together these concepts produce two simple lessons. First, it is no longer physically possible to externalize the environmental costs and damages outside the production process and allow them to be borne by nature and future generations: industrial processes and products must be redesigned to internalize such costs and damages within the production and consumption processes. Second, it is no longer possible to externalize the human and social costs and damages associated with economic growth and technological development outside of the richest social groups. New and more balanced mechanisms for the production, monitoring, and distribution of wealth among groups, generations, countries, and regions will be required.

The finite nature of the world does not mean a reduction in the density and scope of interdependence and uncertainty. The finite limits of development at the global level require that our societies must learn to cope with a higher degree of complexity than did a world based on the nation-state system, the national economy and culture, and national history.

Managing complexity in a finite world is not a process that should be taken for granted. The problems and challenges characterizing the present transition highlight the fact that our societies are not fully equipped to manage the complexities of differing natures and at various levels. Although we are used to complexity (we face it every day at all levels of action), we must now learn how to respond to the problems and challenges of a system operating at a higher level of complexity than in the past. Developing new methods of learning, goal setting, and decisionmaking (and hence a new generation of more participatory instruments and mechanisms) is unavoidable.[12] The question of nation-state sovereignty comes to the fore of the debate. In an epoch characterized by growing complexity, the principle of national sovereignty is becoming outdated.[13]

## The Emergence of a Global Civil Society

It is within the context described above, as well as in relation to other phenomena that will be examined later (such as the explosion of ethnic and religious conflicts, the increase in poverty, and the crisis of megacities) that another element of the global world has been developing rapidly: global civil society. This society is an ensemble of all those organized social groups and institutions (voluntary associations, nonprofit organizations, nongovernmental organizations, or NGOs) that act at the local, national, and global level, in all spheres of human activity, to improve individual and collective social conditions.[14]

Global civil society is a complicated galaxy. It is composed of thousands of organized groups and institutions that deal with issues such as the promotion of nonviolence, the preservation of endangered animal species, the defense and promotion of equal opportunities for women, the fight against animal vivisection, nature conservation, the ecology movement, the dialogue among religions, the fight against torture, the defense of immigrants, the development of new forms of economic activities, the strengthening of transnational cooperation between minority languages, and the search for new ethics in business and in technological development. Global civil society is an expression of the high moral and human-inspired standards of social advocacy in today's world. The form and content of this activism are diverse. They encompass a variety of movements including Greenpeace, the Association against Racism and Xenophobia, the Red Cross, and the World Wildlife Fund. The degree of activism also varies considerably: some groups and organizations, for example Amnesty International and the United States—originated Friends of the Earth, have become rather professionalized. Some are true multinational organizations employing hundreds of people on a permanent basis throughout the world. Others remain spontaneous entities, using modes of action and intervention based on a purely voluntary goodwill commitment. Of course, the availability of financial resources plays an important role. The difference between rich organizations such as the World Wildlife Fund and the very modest International Association for the Defense of Minority Languages is as vast as the difference between prosperous Japan and poor Burkina Faso.

Global civil society is characterized by a high degree of concentration in a few areas such as the environmental movement, North-South development relations, and human rights. Daily life demonstrates that it is not easy to set up and maintain at transnational and global levels effective coordination policies and mechanisms among a large number of culturally diversified organizations. The 1992 United Nations Conference on Environment and Development in Rio de Janeiro showed, among other things, that global civil society was still quite fragmented, uncoordinated, and divided from within (cleavages included North vs. South; environmentalists vs. developmentalists; reformism vs. revolutionary militantism; localists vs. globalists; and progovernment forces vs. those advocating active autonomy).[15]

Much depends on the history of the emergence and development of the specific components of the transnational civil society, as well as on the national context. In some countries, such as the United States, Mexico, Brazil, the United Kingdom, Sweden, the Netherlands, and Italy, voluntary associations have a long tradition. This is not the case in France, for instance, where the movement has been heavily influenced and constrained by the omnipresent role of the state; nor in Japan, for different reasons. The same applies in most countries of Africa, Latin America, and Asia, where the state continues to play the principal role in organizing and mobilizing the national/local communities and resources. The tendency of many associations to transform themselves into businesslike enterprises that increasingly obey financial logic and managerial constraints has become a source of concern inside and outside the world of voluntary and nongovernmental associations.

Despite such developments, global civil society plays a historically important role with regard to three basic functions. First, it acts as the emerging planetary moral consciousness. Universally oriented religions may also be considered expressions of global moral consciousness. Yet it is the transnational civil society that acts as the promoter of the moral ideas and prescriptions contained in the Universal Charter of Human Rights. If this galaxy of interests did not exist, it would be difficult to identify who was the planetary voice today for the good, the beautiful and just. It is certainly not global markets that represent such a voice.

Second, this galaxy is able to shape and express global needs, aspirations, and objectives, that is, what we call global social demand. In many respects the galaxy speaks for the world concerning human development, freedom, peace, equality, harmony, solidarity, and justice. The social demand expressed by a multitude of organizations relates to social justice, human dignity, political democracy, economic well-being, community development, cultural identity, and freedom. This demand is centered on practical matters and issues: the fight against famine and hunger in the world; the improvement of women's conditions at work, at home, and in public life; the preservation of ecological equilibria; the fight against the depletion of the ozone layer; the reduction of poverty, social exclusion, and intolerance with a view to eradicating the main causes of ethnic and interstate wars.

The galaxy successfully applied pressure on national governments and United Nations organizations to convene the Rio Conference. This conference was not conceived of or desired by the superpowers. The United States, for instance, was reluctant to participate, and the president confirmed his attendance only a few days before the opening, after he obtained a guarantee that U. S. negotiation objectives would be met. Multinational corporations and trade unions did not take up the initiative either. The Rio Conference was promoted by voluntary associations and NGOs, following the U.N. environment conference in Stockholm in 1972. It found a natural ally in the United Nations system, which made possible its implementation. The existence of such a social demand is promising because it represents the basis—though confused, weak, and fragile for the time being—for explicit and tacit negotiations at the world level on a global social contract. The Rio Conference represented a remarkable achievement because it was the first truly global negotiation on the wealth of the world. The issue, in fact, was how to create the conditions necessary for the sustainable development of a world economy that can reconcile the high level of quality of life in the developed countries with the solution to the quantity-type problems of direct concern to the billions of people in less-developed and poor countries.

The result of the conference, Agenda 21, contains the commitment made at the Earth Summit by the governments and political leaders of more than 120 countries.[16] Some deem the negotiations a qualified failure given the number and scope of formal conventions originally expected to be signed. But the conference took place; and lessons have been learned for the future. One lesson is especially encouraging: not only are negotiations useful when they have to solve opposing interests such as the case of negotiations at the General Agreement on Tariffs and Trade (GATT) level, but world negotiations on common problems and projects can also take place. A new perspective has therefore been developed by the Rio Conference.

This leads to the third basic function of global civil society, that is, the offer of a global capacity for politically innovative behavior. Global civil society is not only a moral consciousness, nor is it simply limited to expressing needs and aspirations. Because of its multiform and multilevel ability to act, it also contributes to the solution of problems. It allows us the opportunity to experience new ways of coping with issues and challenges, and to identify new institutional, economic, and social solutions. Among the many examples, one can quote the work of Amnesty International and the big effort among Mexican, U.S., and Canadian groups who, during the free trade treaty debate, negotiated a more equitable and sustainable trade initiative for North America. National governmental authorities, although still the predominant agents, must now contend with groups (often quite powerful) that are working around them, and are forming their own regional, international, and global links. These groups often advocate the establishment of limits to economic competition among firms and among nations. In this sense, they can modify the single-minded, interest-based calculations of national governments and multinational corporations.

Until now this function has been made possible by the numerous international organizations that comprise the United Nations system. These have gradually associated the NGOs and voluntary associations with their activities, so that today transnational civil society is mostly identified with the successes and failures of the United Nations system.

The global civil society that we have described is the most visible and organized component of the new global world, but it is not the only one. Another important component of this society is the new global enlightened elites to which we have previously referred in discussing the development of a communications village. These elites are composed of social groups and organizations originating mainly from North America, Western Europe, and Southeast Asia, with a minority coming from Africa, Russia, Latin America, and the rest of Asia. They are represented by the generation of industrialists, business leaders, and managers who are working to build up the global networks of multinational firms, and who design and implement global strategies for new world products, infrastructures, norms/standards, services, and markets with a humanistic vision and a great sense of social responsibility vis-à-vis present and future generations.

Their value system has adopted concepts such as global competitiveness, global leadership, global efficiency, and global thinking as their own. They are sensitive to quality (rather than quantity), diversity (rather than homogenization), Toyotism (rather than Fordism), and the need to reduce hierarchical structures within their own organizations. They pay increasing attention to human factors, cultural identity, and specificity. The enlightened elites also include the new generation of politicians and civil servants who have by and large adhered to the liberal, market-economy ideology without becoming prisoners of the extreme form that it took under the influence of Reaganism and Thatcherism. They are the neoliberal social democrats of the world. They have been the primary participants in the establishment and development of the Bretton Woods and United Nations systems and the rich web of intergovernmental organizations. Large segments of the intelligentsia, the media, trade unions, and the arts also form a component of the new enlightened transnational elites.

The members of this new elite have received comparable education and training in the northern universities and colleges. They speak the same language not only in linguistic terms (Anglo-American) but also in cultural terms (that is, they share to a large extent the same values and views on many economic, social, and world issues). Culturally and politically, they form what we call the center of the global world order that they are building and managing. The enlightened elites are aware that the basic principles, goals, modalities, and results of the old industrial modernization processes are no longer valid. They recognize, for instance, that the industrial growth of the last century has posed an ecological threat to this century. They realize that quantitative growth cannot be maintained as the primary objective of innovation and the use of material and nonmaterial resources. Also, they understand that increasing the efficiency of the economy cannot be the only target of R&D, management, and organizational behavior. The same applies to price competition—the importance of which is increasingly overshadowed by competition on product quality and variety. They are also aware that new processes and policies for a new type of growth and economic modernization must be designed to counter the increasingly high level of unemployment in the OECD countries and the spread of poverty across the world.

An example of the new enlightened elites is represented by the Business Council for Sustainable Development (in Switzerland), created by the Swiss industrialist Stephan Schmidheiny, which produced *Changing Course*[17] in 1992. This is a strong and well-reasoned manifesto that supports the concept of sustainable development proposed by the Brundtland Commission in *Our Common Future*.

## The Reorganization of the World Economy and Society

Despite the importance of global imagery and the infrastructure of information and communications technologies, they are not the primary forces in the making of the global world. Nor are they the discriminating factors that will influence individual and collective choices toward the construction of a balanced, integrated, and cooperative global world, or of a fragmented, conflictual, and competitive type of global world. The primary creators of the global world are people, their value systems, and the means they employ to achieve their goals. Global civil society is an example of these actors as well as the financial and industrial forces supporting the new networks of global firms.

The global world in the making is the result of the flow of ideas, aspirations, strategies, resources, and goods—as well as norms, rules, and institutions that people put into action to influence and control events. In this sense, globalization is an entirely new process.

**Globalization, Internationalization, and Multinationalization**
Although the concepts of internationalization, multinationalization, and globalization are generally used in an indistinct and often confusing way, they refer to different processes and phenomena. More important, they imply different actors, playing the game by different rules, and they have significantly different impacts on strategies, policies, and societies.[18] Therefore globalization is a new phenomenon in comparison to internationalization and multinationalization.

The internationalization of economy and society refers to the flow of raw materials, semifinished and finished products and services, money, ideas, and people between two or more nation-states. Compiling trade and migration statistics is the most common method of measuring and monitoring the nature, scope, and direction of internationalization. For thousands of years, people have traded goods and services across nations and have moved from country to country, with or without coercion. In modern national capitalism, internationalization evolved through the establishment of colonies and the rise of mercantilism. In 1972 George Modelski used the term globalization to refer explicitly to European-led expansion to gain control over other communities in the world and to integrate these into one global trading system.[19] The same interpretation was behind the French expression *economie-monde* used by the historian Ferdinand Braudel[20] in his great *fresque* on the emergence of capitalism.

Over the centuries, the pattern and degree of internationalization has changed, as old powers have given way to new ones with different interests and strategies. However, as soon as a new state took over the reins of colonial conquest and expansion of trade, new theories and doctrines were developed to account for these changes and to justify the underlying power relationships. Thus, at a time when the United Provinces rose to a position of dominance in world trade, the Dutch scholar Grotius developed his legal doctrine declaring the freedom of the world oceans, which was intended to defy the Spanish-Portuguese division of the oceans sanctioned by the Pope.[21] Likewise, Ricardo's theory of comparative cost advantages was used to sustain British commercial superiority throughout the nineteenth century and U.S. superiority after World War II—with some necessary revisions as codified by the Bretton Woods agreements. The same holds true today. As correctly pointed out by Winfried Ruigrok and Rob van Tulder, Ohmae's

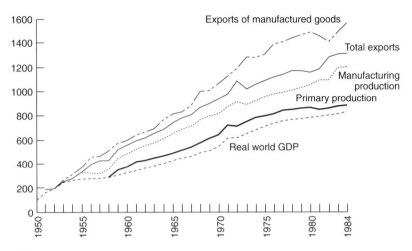

**Figure 1.1**
World exports and production
Source: GATT, *International Trade 1986*, Geneva, 1987.

globalization theory "serves to rationalise the internationalization/globaliza-
tion of Japanese firms just like Vernon's product life cycle model rationalized
U.S. multinationalization."[22]

The internationalization of economy and society is based on national
actors. An important role is played by national public authorities. They
direct and control the flows of exchange via the monetary instruments,
taxation, fiscal policy, public procurement markets, norms and standards,
and movements of people. They make decisions on national citizenship as
well as on closing and opening national borders.

In the context of the internationalization of the economy, competition
among enterprises from the different national economies is a crucial instrument in ensuring and maintaining positive sectoral trade balances. Liberal-
izing the flows of exchange has been the driving ideology of the last fifty
years and of the GATT, the institutional organization set up to promote and
safeguard the liberalization of trade relations at the international level.
Figure 1.1 depicts the steady growth of the internationalization of the
economy since the 1950s.

The multinationalization of economy and society is characterized fundamentally by the transfer and relocalization of resources, especially capital—

and to a lesser extent labor—from one national economy to another. A typical form of multinationalization in the economy is the development of a firm's production capacities in another country via direct subsidiaries, acquisitions, or various types of cooperation (commercial, financial, technological, and industrial) (see figure 1.2). Economic multinationalization conforms to the logic of expanding the market dimension, which ensures that the optimal combination of factors of production does not occur any longer within national borders, but is increasingly dictated by the mechanisms and processes that imply a multiterritorialization (multinationalization) of product activities.[23]

The theory of the international division of labor is no longer entirely adequate to explain the behavior of firms and the overall functioning of the economy. Business and management theories are more useful in analyzing the acquisition and control of market shares and profit maximization by the firm in its own interest as the driving forces behind multinationalization.[24] Through multinationalization, an economic agent from a foreign country develops the capacity to exert influence on a given nation's economy or future. This is why—contrary to internationalization processes—multinationalization has very often been the subject of economic protection and nationalistic cultural/political reaction. Fears of and opposition to the presence of foreign-owned enterprises and foreign investments have consistently accompanied the massive or strategically selected presence of multinational firms (especially American). Today this fear often takes the form of "Japanophobia." The United States and many European and Asian countries are concerned about the rapid penetration of Japanese firms into an increasing number of important sectors of their economies.

National governments find themselves supporting their national firms in their search for effective multinationalization, both in offensive terms (that is, by actively supporting the competitive strength of their multinational firms) and in defensive terms (by creating obstacles to the penetration of foreign multinational firms into their national territory). Among the many other instruments available, antitrust regulations are, under these circumstances, a powerful tool in protecting the national economy and domestic firms against the power of competitive foreign firms. Of course, firms protest all forms of protectionism when they are strong players and believe they can win. They do not reject protection from their government, however, when they feel themselves to be weak and at risk of losing.

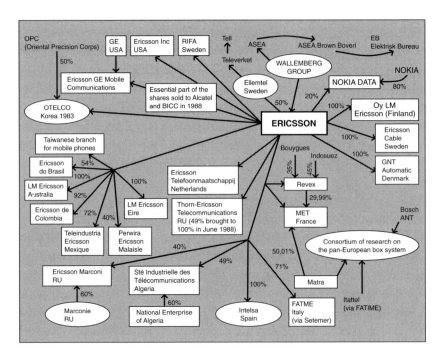

**Figure 1.2**
Ericsson in the world, an example of economic multinationalization

On a broader scale, the multinationalization of society implies that social agents (a university, a newspaper, a church, a trade union, a social institution) or a process (the education system, modes of life, value systems) are capable of expanding and installing themselves in other national contexts and transforming them from the inside, while maintaining their own uniqueness. Conversely, they are subject to influence, transformation, and control from other national agents. All in all, national agents, institutions, and processes are increasingly moved to enter into a multinational-based process of coexistence and codevelopment. To express such a movement, concepts like transnationalization are appropriate.

The globalization of economy and society is a recent phenomenon, and the forms and processes that it takes vary tremendously. Some may disappear or lose their relevance in ten to fifteen years. National factors continue to affect how globalization can transform the national economy and society.

There is no single model of globalization. This is why it has been difficult to find a commonly accepted definition.[25]

One may discern several processes of globalization:

- of finance;
- of markets and strategies, in particular, competition;
- of technology and related R&D and knowledge;
- of modes of life and consumption patterns, with extension to the globalization of culture;
- of regulatory capabilities and governance;
- as the political unification of the world;
- of perception and consciousness.

Table 1.3 summarizes present concepts and actual processes of globalization. None of these types of globalization, however, expresses the paradigm of the nature and features of globalization. None of their main theoreticians therefore can claim to possess a greater truth than the others.

The changes that have occurred in the last fifteen to twenty years are so great in so many fields (finance, communications networks, infrastructures, enterprise organization, regulatory frameworks, transport, flows of goods of perception and consciousness. and services, consumption patterns, value systems, the role of nation-states, population growth, geopolitics) that concepts such as internationalization and multinationalization prove inadequate to describe what is happening and why. The increasing use of new concepts such as globalization is not due to fashion alone. It expresses the need to understand processes that have lost their visibility and meaning in terms of traditional concepts. Of course not all theories of globalization are equally pertinent or justifiable, nor is it enough to make a syncretic fusion of them to obtain the ultimate truth. Our definition is closer to the one proposed by McGrew and his colleagues:

Globalization refers to the multiplicity of linkages and interconnections between the states and societies which make up the present world system. It describes the process by which events, decisions, and activities in one part of the world come to have significant consequences for individuals and communities in quite distant parts of the globe. Globalization has two distinct phenomena: scope (or stretching) and intensity (or deepening). On the one hand, it defines a set of processes which embrace most of the globe or which operate worldwide; the concept therefore has a spatial connotation. On the other hand it also implies an intensification in the levels of interaction,

**Table 1.3**
Concepts of globalization

| Category | Main elements/processes |
| --- | --- |
| 1. Globalization of finances and capital ownership. | Deregulation of financial markets, international mobility of capital, rise of mergers and acquisitions. The globalization of shareholding is at its initial stage. |
| 2. Globalization of markets and strategies. | Integration of business activities on a worldwide scale, establishment of integrated operations abroad (incl. R&D and financing) , search for components, strategic alliances. |
| 3. Globalization of technology and linked R&D and knowledge. | Technology is the primary enzyme: the rise of information technology and telecommunications enables the rise of global networks within the same firm, and between different firms. Globalization as the process of universalization of Toyotism/lean production. |
| 4. Globalization of modes of life and consumption patterns; globalization of culture. | Transfer and transplantation of predominant modes of life. Equalization of consumption patterns. The role of the media. Transformation of culture in "cultural food," "cultural products." GATT rules applied to cultural flows. |
| 5. Globalization of regulatory capabilities and governance. | The diminished role of national governments and parliaments. Attempts to design a new generation of rules and institutions for global governance. |
| 6. Globalization as the political unification of the world. | State-centered analysis of the integration of world societies into a global political and economic system led by a core power. |
| 7. Globalization of perception and consciousness. | Sociocultural processes as centered on "One Earth," the "globalist" movement, planetary citizenship. |

Source: Broadened and revised table based on W. Ruigrok and R. van Tulder, *The Ideology of Interdependence*, Ph.D. diss., University of Amsterdam, June 1993.

interconnectedness or interdependence between the states and societies which constitute the world community. Accordingly, alongside the stretching goes a deepening of global processes. . . . Far from being an abstract concept, globalization articulates one of the more familiar features of modern existence. . . . Of course, globalization does not mean that the world is becoming more politically united, economically interdependent or culturally homogeneous. Globalisation is highly uneven in its scope and highly differentiated in its consequences.[26]

Current forms of globalization do not imply that it is the "right" process and as such deserves political support and cultural adhesion. Nor does globalization imply that the prerequisites and ongoing constraints in current forms of globalization are the ones that have to be accepted and respected. In fact, most of the dominant features of contemporary globalization raise rather serious concerns because of the problems they have already begun to create and for the undesirable consequences that they will produce in the future if current forms of globalization remain predominant.

## From National to Global Capitalism

In our view, the meaning of the new global world is that all of our futures are made in the world. The process of globalization is the beginning of the end of the national system as the apex of human-organized activities and strategies. For centuries now, our societies have been characterized by the predominance of national dynamics: the nation-state has been considered the ultimate form of political organization of society; national identity determined the personality of individuals and social groups; the national economy has been considered the only coherent and integrated form of economy. National history (e.g., a nation's language, culture, railway system, education system, sports teams, sovereignty, democracy) has been the central process of human society. Every process was defined in relation to the national dimension—upward (international, multinational, supranational, transnational) and downward (intranational, subnational, infranational).

Today, nation-states still exist. In some cases, the process of nation-state building has even been accelerated as the result of decolonization and the recent emergence of new nation-states following the collapse of the Soviet Union. It would be an oversimplification, however, to suggest that the nation-state is a form of political organization that is too small to respond to the growing number of global problems and challenges and too big to cope with local issues and solutions.[27] The problem lies elsewhere, in the pretension of the nation-state to be the central and often the only player in global affairs. One area where the pretensions of nation-state sovereignty present a major source of difficulty is that of environmental protection and management. In just a few hours, the Chernobyl explosions highlighted the vast gap between the theoretical and political model of state sovereignty and the technological and environmental reality of the biosphere.[28]

Equally, although national languages and cultures have not lost their importance, they are no longer considered exclusive or ultimate form of individual and collective cultural ingenuity and expression. Multilingualism and cross-cultural development are becoming assets, goals to achieve, positive societal constructions. Many other examples can be given. True, the nation continues to be one of the levels of relevance, but it is no longer the main strategic level for the key actors in the areas of scientific development, technological innovation, and socioeconomic growth.[29]

The increasing globalization of the economy is eroding one of the basic foundations of the nation-state, that is, the national market. The national space is being replaced as the most relevant strategic economic area by the nascent global space. This does not mean that the power of the nation-state—in particular its military power—is declining, or that nation-states are being replaced in the economic sphere by transnational firms because the latter are, according to some authors, more democratic than the former.[30] Nor does it mean that the national economy, as such, has lost its importance. In many instances, the opposite is true, especially regarding the less-developed economies of recently created nation-states. The economic fight for global leadership among the most developed national economies of the world (e.g., Germany, the United States, Japan, France, Italy, and the United Kingdom) also suggests that the national economy is still quite operational. But it is no longer the name of the game. The production of wealth, for example, in Germany, France, Japan, Finland, or Costa Rica is no longer dependent on the performance of their local firms' technology, capital, and labor, but rather relies on firms that are increasingly part of global networks of financial and industrial corporations that respond to strategic interests that are not bound to German, French, Japanese, Finnish, or Costa Rican national interests. It is even more dependent on technology designed and produced elsewhere in the world, on capital made available at the global level (as shown by the fast-growing globalization of financial and capital markets) and, increasingly, on highly skilled labor not necessarily trained in their own country.[31]

For decades, and in some cases a couple of centuries, the industrial economy and modernization have essentially been the history of a national industry. The rise and growth of national capitalism have expressed the sense and direction of the historical processes. Although it would be wrong to declare the death of national capitalism, it is true that national capitalism has ceased to be the only coherent form of organizing capital, and its predominance will rapidly disappear in the coming decades. The history of capitalism has ceased to be defined by and limited to national boundaries. A new epoch, the era of global capitalism, is developing rapidly and will influence the evolution of our societies in the decades to come.[32]

The world has not entered the postcapitalist era. The ownership and, more important, the control of the mobilization of capital for the most efficient use of the world's available material and nonmaterial resources remains the dominant factor of economic and sociopolitical power. The emerging break is not between a capitalist and a postcapitalist society, nor between "good" capitalism (the social market economy) and "bad" capitalism (the jungle, the "casino" market economy).[33] Rather it is between a weakening national capitalism and a growing global capitalism. This shift reflects a nascent historical change: the world is slowly starting to move away from the era of the wealth of nations to the era of the wealth of the world.

### Capital Flows: The Primary Enzymes of Global Capitalism

The liberalization of the movement of capital across countries, particularly since 1971 when Richard Nixon declared the nonconvertibility of the U.S. dollar, was one of the most important factors that accelerated the shift toward global capitalism and the wealth of the world. Capital flows comprise three main categories:

• monetary and financial flows, linked to the trade of goods and services (for example, import/export transactions, tourism expenditures);

• foreign direct investment, which not only implies financial capital transfers but also transfers of physical, human, and technological capital;

• portfolio investments and various types of financial transactions (including speculative operations).

The globalization of capital flows has been the nerve center of the globalization of the economy.[34]

Whereas capital flows at the world level exhibited a relative atrophy from the end of World War II until the end of 1960s—coinciding to a large extent with the period of national reconstructions—the 1970s witnessed a rapid acceleration and intensification of the globalization of financial markets. In the view of Aglietta and his colleagues, the financial globalization that took place in the 1970s was characterized by the transfer of surplus capital from the OPEC countries to the poor developing countries, mediated by the banks from the Northern countries. During this period the Northern countries profited by using the capital (petrodollars) of a part of the South to finance the development of the rest of the South. In fact, the poor countries of the South entered into the vicious cycle of debt while the oil-rich countries of the South financed the economic and financial betterment of the North.[35]

In the 1980s another major change occurred. South-South (via North) capital flows were replaced by North-North flows, and in particular, as shown in figures 1.3 and 1.4, by capital flows within the triad (that is, the three richest regions of the North-Japan and the "four dragons," Western Europe, and the United States). More than 80 percent of world flows either originate from or go to the three regions of the triad. The role played by the less-developed countries or LDCs as originators of flows has been reduced to zero in 1989 from about 14 percent in 1982 (figure 1.3). There was a timid recovery in 1989 in terms of countries of destination of capital flows.

More recent data confirms the situation for the period 1989–1990. The triadization of capital flows during the 1980s was marked by the fast-growing role played by Japan compared to that of Europe and the United States. The reason was rather simple. Whereas the 1970s centered on the recycling of OPEC surpluses, the 1980s centered on the recycling of Japanese surpluses. Of course, the process took place almost exclusively in the OECD countries, and Japan's ability to steer it has proved to be quite

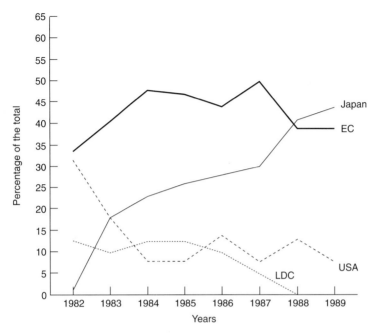

**Figure 1.3**
International capital flows according to their origin (not including the reserves and operations of international organizations)
Source: IMF.

adequate. The result was that from 1986 to 1989, Japan represented on average 26.93 percent of total world capital flows—far above the United States (16.41 percent). Also, between 1984 and 1988, 64 percent of Japanese trade loans, 70 percent of direct investments abroad, and 86 percent of portfolio investments (95.5 percent in 1988) went to the two other regions of the triad.[36]

The current global economy can best be described by one expression: delinking of less-developed countries. Since 1980, the new global world created and shaped by capital flows has been accompanied by the marginalization of most LDCs. The entire group of LDCs in 1980 attracted about 55 percent of world capital flows and was itself the source of 14 percent of the outgoing flows. Ten years later, both percentages had dropped dramatically, declining to 2 percent. If one excludes those LDCs that have become

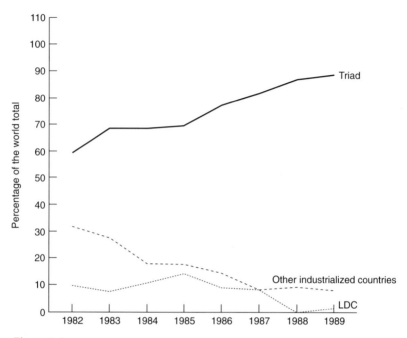

**Figure 1.4**
International capital flows according to their destination (not including the reserves
and operations of international organizations)
Source: IMF.

major offshore financial centers (Panama, Hong Kong, the Cayman Islands,
and the Dutch Caribbean islands) and the capital flows from international
organizations and public donations, the result is that the total investment and
loans both of a public and private nature that went to the less-developed and
poor countries of the world represented less than 3 percent of world flows
between 1986 and 1991. The gradual exclusion of the largest majority of
LDCs is particularly striking with regard to industrial and financial investments and international bank loans. Starting in 1982, there has been a brutal
halt to the growth of international bank loans destined for the LDCs. Again,
if countries such as Hong Kong, South Korea, Taiwan, Singapore, Thailand,
China, and Turkey are excluded, the very bulk of the LDCs no longer
attracts any capital outside of public donations and multilateral aid. The

capital flows going to these countries are due more to humanitarian actions than to economic logic.

This form of delinking raises a crucial question: How will the global world evolve in the future? Will a new economic logic influence the process of globalization in such a way that the wealth of the world will be the result of all countries' creativity and contributions? A discussion of this question can be found in chapter 3. "Made in the world" is the central concept that highlights the novelty of the current process of globalization.

## Made in the World

From an economic point of view, which is the one that at present enables quantification, the new phenomenon of globalization is an ensemble of processes:

- that make possible the design, development, production, distribution, and consumption of processes, products, and services on a worldwide scale, using instruments made available on a worldwide basis (such as patents, data bases, new information, communication, and transport technologies and infrastructures);
- that are geared toward satisfying increasingly diversified and customized global markets regulated by quasi-universal norms and standards;
- that are based on organizations (networks of firms) acting on a worldwide basis, whose capital is (increasingly) owned by a multiplicity of shareholders from different countries, whose culture is open to a world context and obeys a world strategy. It is difficult to identify the specific territoriality (legal, economic, technological) of these organizations, although they somehow have a home base, owing to the intensive forms of interrelationships and integration that occur among firms, infrastructures, and rules at the various phases of the conception, production, distribution, and consumption of goods and services.

Credit cards are a typical example of a global service devised for a specialized, high-value-added world market, based on the integration of whole clusters of new technologies (data processing, materials, telecommunications) and managed by globalized organizations with growing world expertise. The car is a typical example of a global product. The car is no longer "made in the USA," "made in France," or "made in Japan," but is often "made in the world." This applies not only to the production side, but more important, to the whole system that facilitates the production, marketing, and sales of about 30 million cars per year. The globalization of the car industry is in its initial stage. The processes of internationalization and multinationalization are still in the expansion phase. Regarding internationalization processes, the opening of each country vis-à-vis import penetration ratios in the 1980s has been strongly affected by the national regulatory environment. Many governments have sought primarily political answers to the "threat" of Japanese exporters, which affected the import penetration ratios of Japanese cars. Italian and French imports originate mainly from other European countries, including reimportations of Spanish- or Belgian-made Renaults. The Japanese car complex is heavily dependent on the world market for its exports but hardly at all for its imports. Simply on the basis of this data, it is easy to understand the Japanese government's trade policy strategy: promote a liberal international trade regime, yet ensure that such a regime will not lead to a dramatic rise in imports.

Regarding multinationalization processes, the two largest car producers, Ford and GM, have made the most significant progress: only 42 percent and 58 percent respectively of their production was domestic in 1988. Except for Volvo (57 percent), all large European car makers have over 60 percent of production concentrated in their domestic market and over 80 percent in Europe. The Japanese car complexes also produced most of their cars in Japan and in other parts of Asia, with the exception of Honda. Toyota and Nissan, however, are making rapid progress in this direction. Notwithstanding these phenomena, the globalization of the car sector and its players at the organizational, behavioral, and strategic levels is growing in importance. Of tremendous importance is the explosion of interfirm strategic alliances (see table 1.4), which in the last fifteen years has significantly modified the internal structures of the car sector and, to an even greater degree, other sectors of the economy. The main reasons motivating firms to cooperate with each other are:

- reducing and sharing of costs for R&D;
- ensuring access to complementary technology;
- capturing a partner's tacit knowledge and technology (technological leapfrogging);
- shortening product life cycle;

**Table 1.4**

Summary of major strategic alliances between the key players in the car industry

| Alliance players | Joint R & D | Production consortium | Joint venture | Direct investment minority share | OEM agreement | Distribution | Merger and acquisition |
|---|---|---|---|---|---|---|---|
| BMW | Mercedes, VW, PSA, Renault, Fiat | | | | | | |
| VW | Mercedes, BMW, PSA, Renault, Fiat | Ford, Nissan, Renault | Ford | | Volvo, Rover | Scania | Seat, Skoda |
| Mercedes | VW, PSA, Renault, BMW, Fiat, VW | | Mitsubishi | Bajaj Tempo (India) | Steyr-Damler, Puch | Mitsubishi | |
| Fiat | Mercedes, VW, PSA, Renault, BMW, Volvo, Rover | | | VDT | S-D-Puch, Premier Automobiles | Chrysler | Alfa Romeo, Ferrari |
| Rover | VW, PSA, Renault, Volvo, Fiat | Honda | Honda | | Hindustan, Honda, Renault, VW, PSA | Honda, PSA, Suzuki | |
| PSA | Mercedes, VW, BMW, Renault, Fiat, Volvo | Renault | Renault | Renault | Ford, Rover | Mazda, Rover, Suzuki | |
| Renault | Mercedes, VW, PSA, Fiat, BMW, Volvo, Rover | VW, PSA, Volvo, Toyota | PSA | Volvo | Chrysler, Volvo, Rover, S-D-Puch | Chrysler, Volvo | |
| Volvo | PSA | Mitsubishi | | Renault | Mitsubishi, VW, Renault | Puji Heavy, Renault | |
| Chrysler | Mitsubishi, Ford, GM | GM, Hyundai, Mitsubishi | Mitsubishi, Fiat, S-D-Puch | Mitsubishi, Mahindra | Mitsubishi, Renault | Mitsubishi, Renault | Lamborghini |
| GM | Ford, Chrysler | Chrysler, Toyota | Suzuki, Toyota | Isuzu, Suzuki, Daewoo | Isuzu, Suzuki, Hindustan, S-D-Puch | Isuzu, Suzuki | Lotus, Saab |
| Ford | General Motors, Chrysler | VW, Nissan, Mazda | VW | Mazda, Kia | PSA | Mazda, Kia | AAC Cars, Jaguar, AM Lagonda |
| Honda | | Rover | | Rover | S-D-Puch, Rover | Rover | |
| Mazda | S-D-Puch | Ford | | Kia, JATCO, Ford | Suzuki, Ford, Kia | Kia, PSA, Fiat | |
| Mitsubishi | Chrysler | Chrysler, Volvo | Chrysler, Mercedes | Chrysler, Hyundai | Chrysler, Volvo | Chrysler, Mercedes | |
| Nissan | Fuji Heavy | VW, Ford | | JATCO, Mahindra | Puji, Premier | | |
| Toyota | | GM, Hino, Renault | GM | Daihatsu, Hino | | | |

Source: W. Ruigrok and H. van Tulder, "The Internationalisation of the Economy: Global Strategies and Strategic Technology Alliances," *Nouvelles de la Science et des Technologies* vol. 9, no. 2, Brussels, 1991.

- sharing costs in product development;
- securing access to foreign markets;
- having access to highly qualified people;
- gaining access to financial resources.[37]

Thus an increasing number of products are designed jointly by several firms. Their engineers work together on the same idea for years at a time. Similarly, the phases or elements in the production process comprising a growing number of components enable firms in different countries to collaborate. Interfirm strategic alliances are what they say the term implies: different firms sharing their strategies with others, even if—as is the case for the majority of the alliances—their hidden hope or intention is to absorb their partner. This is their contribution to the process reflected in the phrase "made in the world." The phenomenon of interfirm strategic alliances is fairly new; it exploded onto the world scene in the 1980s.[38] Though it has been particularly rapid and intense in the new technology-based industries (computers, telecommunications), all sectors have been affected (see figure 1.5).

Strategic alliances are destined to expand even further in the future. As was the case in the last fifteen years, not all alliances will have a happy end. The expansion will also be marked by pitfalls, failures, and disappointments. Some will remain just good intentions, events covered by the media worldwide, such as the aborted mega-alliance between Bell Atlantic and MCI. Experience also suggests that interfirm strategic alliances are not always moved by a genuine spirit of cooperation. Short-term opportunistic motives and the aggressive search for financial and economic power are sharply influencing this phenomenon.[39] Nevertheless, the process leading to greater integration of national and multinational firms into global networks of firms by means of mergers, acquisitions, and interfirm strategic alliances is destined to continue and likely to accelerate, especially in some industries: computers, telecommunications, media, shipbuilding, construction, leisure, and civil air transportation. One may easily expect that in ten to fifteen years it will be difficult to identify who does what, and which part of the network is related to this segment or that production center of a given firm. Already a new phenomenon has emerged, that is, the "virtual corporation." Virtual corporations are ephemeral corporations created to finance very costly research or the development of a product, and are then dissolved.[40]

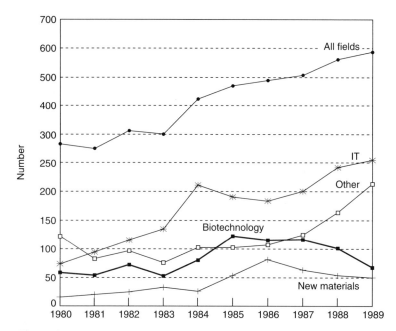

**Figure 1.5**
Growth of newly established strategic technology alliances in core technologies and other fields, 1980–1989

Source: John Hagedoorn and Jan Schakenraad, *The Role of Interfirm Cooperation Agreements in the Globalization of Economy and Technology*, FAST, Commission of the European Communities, Brussels, November 1991.

"Made in the world" is also the result of an even stronger component process of globalization, namely foreign direct investment (FDI). For example, between 1983 and 1989 world exports increased by 9.4 percent a year and the average annual growth of world gross domestic product was 7.8 percent, while annual foreign direct investment grew by 28.9. According to a report on FDI by the former United Nations Center on Transnational Corporations, "international transactions are increasingly dominated by transnational corporations. . . . One implication of such a development is that the global patterns of trade, technology transfers and private financial flows could tend to converge on the foreign direct investment patterns, making the latter a principal force in the structuring of the world economy."[41]

FDI is the genuine form of the mobility of capital and therefore of the globalization of capitalism. It has been at the center of the multinationalization process since the last century (as in the case of the creation of production facilities in Latin America by the German chemical industry). But FDI is not always the instrument of globalization. When a European firm buys an American company, the result is an increase in the concentration of production activity in Europe and the United States under the ownership or control of the European firm. For instance, the fact that (if present forecasts are correct) the number of global players in the telecommunications industry will be reduced by half the current number in 2010 through mergers and acquisitions will not lead to a higher level of globalization in the industry, but to a drastic acceleration in the process of concentration of financial and industrial structures at the world level in that sector.

Foreign direct investments have important political consequences. For years, Europeans have held the lead. They remain the principal originators of FDI, but Japanese FDI is constantly gaining ground as Japanese multinational corporations extend their presence abroad. Without doubt, since the 1970s advanced capitalism has been actively globalizing to include America, Japan, Korea, Singapore, and Western Europe. The process is accelerating. If opportunity costs change, the decision can be taken to close factory X in country A and open a new one making the same products in country B. "Made in the world" also takes this rather elusive form.

### Three Engines of Globalization: Liberalization, Privatization, Deregulation

As we have seen in the section devoted to capital flows, liberalization of capital movements was one of the basic factors behind the acceleration and intensification of the globalization of the economy. Making national markets open to free trade and movement of goods, services, people, and capital is one of the sacred commandments of market capitalism. Since Adam Smith's masterpiece *The Wealth of Nations,* the removal of all kinds of tariff and nontariff barriers to international trade is presented as the key political economy prescription on which a sane and prosperous world could be built and operated, according to the liberal market theory.

The entire post–World War II trade system was also based on the philosophy and principles of national market liberalization, thanks to the mechanisms of multilateral negotiations and agreements that the GATT provided for. Starting in 1947, each successive trade round (Dillon, Kennedy, Tokyo, and Uruguay) was intended to expand the process of liberalization of national markets to all sectors. The recently included Uruguay Round was primarily concerned with the liberalization of agriculture, services, and audiovisual goods.

The process of liberalization does not function without difficulties, including sometimes conflicts of interest. Usually it is the strongest economy that is in favor of the most extensive and intensive liberalization of trade and movements of capital, people, and services. Liberalization, however, has created an opposing force—protectionism—which is considered by liberal trade theorists to be the source of most economic illness. In today's world, which is characterized by the predominance of free-market ideology and culture, being accused of practicing any form of protectionism is something that all political and economic leaders will try to avoid. They would rather accuse others of being the guilty ones.

Global liberalization has gained new appeal and apparent legitimization in the last twenty years in connection with the improvement of transport technologies and the explosion of new information and communication technologies (the so-called computer economy and civilization of satellites). The argument is that in a "communication global village," national barriers are creating or maintaining artificially high costs and prices in the interest of noncompetitive producers to the detriment of local consumers. Furthermore, it is argued that it is no longer possible to maintain tariff and nontariff barriers for a growing number of high-tech and knowledge-based goods and services. Information-generated value added cannot be kept within rigid national borders. The debate is ongoing. The authors of the GATT treaties have recognized that negotiated and accepted limits to liberalization of capital flows can be permitted on a temporary basis. Furthermore, not everybody is convinced that limits to free trade are a bad thing per se and that protection of what people consider—via politically accountable democratic procedures—to be in a country's vital interest is an inferior legitimate objective to the politically unaccountable and imperfect functioning of the competitive free market. Today, however, liberalization of national markets is the prevailing approach.

Another interrelated principle and the second engine of the present form of globalization is privatization. Independent from the fight against communism and any form of economic socialism, the drive toward privatization of the mixed economy in the advanced modern societies of the Western world (such as the United States, Canada, Scandinavia, Germany, the Netherlands, Switzerland, and Belgium) has been widely successful since the beginning of 1970s. One after the other, many important sectors of economic activity have been fully or partly privatized on the assumption that the private forces of the market will enable the best allocation of available resources in the best interest of both producers and consumers. Private funding and private investments have been considered the best way to mobilize people's ability and ingenuity in responding to market demands, which continue to be viewed as the best democratic expression of societal needs and the best mechanism for prioritizing them.

To operate in an efficient manner, privatization and national market liberalization require a third element, deregulation. Deregulation has become the third engine of the current globalization process. It has been argued that the state should have only a small direct role in economic activities. State monopolies and state economic intervention, including the establishment of norms and standards, have to be limited. Essentially, market forces are needed to regulate the whole spectrum of functions of the national and international economy at local, regional, and global levels. In many instances, deregulation has been a transitory phase toward full privatization and liberalization. In others, deregulation measures go hand in hand with complementary forms of privatization and liberalization. But few areas have resisted the combined pressure exerted by privatization, deregulation, and liberalization. In every case, the competitiveness imperative was the primary teleological argument used to justify and legitimize such pressure.

Whatever the sector considered (sunrise or sunset; high-tech or low-tech; supply- or demand-oriented; labor- or knowledge-intensive) and the size, strength, and level of development of the country, the argument has been the same: there is an urgent need to privatize to increase the competitiveness of the sector, the firm, and the country in a globalizing economy; there is an urgent need to liberalize all markets to make the local sectors and global-oriented firms more competitive in global markets ; there is an urgent need to deregulate the sector and the markets to enhance the privatization process and hence the competitiveness of local firms and the national (or regional) economy. As these pressures have operated in all sectors and, increasingly, in most countries (including Russia and China), everybody is trying to be competitive in everything against everybody. Under these conditions, the quasi-universal advent of competitive global capitalism as the prescriptive system is not surprising.

## Implications and Consequences

We have only recently begun to rigorously analyze and assess the economic, social, and political implications of the development of a global world. This is due in large part to the availability of more adequate theories of globalization and more reliable data. The present form of globalization is just one—although a major—factor among many that have had an impact on the implications and consequences discussed below.

### Dismantling the Welfare State

The welfare state is based on a written and tacit social contract that guarantees and promotes individual and collective social security, social justice, and effective forms of human and intergenerational solidarity. The welfare state began with the world's first social security measures introduced in Germany by Bismarck in the nineteenth century. It grew as a result of Lord Beveridge's social laws in the United Kingdom after World War I, Roosevelt's New Deal in the United States after the crash of 1929, and the social-democratic regimes developed by the Scandinavian countries after World War II. This social contract has been the basis of the economic, political, and cultural development and well-being of modern industrial society and the nation-state, as well as the enabling environment for growth at relatively low social cost and the acceptance of national capitalism. The form and content of the social contract have varied from country to country within the same region (Western Europe) and among regions (Europe, North America, Japan), but four key issues remain fundamental everywhere (see box 1.1).[42]

Coinciding with the first signs of the economic crisis, which began at the end of the 1960s and lasted until the beginning of the 1970s, the social

**Box 1.1**
The social contract

> The social contract that has been the basis of modern industrial society includes:
>
> - The right to work
>   full employment
>   life-long employment
>   improvement of working conditions (wages, paid leave, weekly working time, workers' participation)
> - The fight against poverty
>   guarantee of a minimum income
>   other forms of social assistance to fight poverty and social exclusion
> - The protection against individual and social risks
>   social security and/or insurance measures to protect the employed and the members of one's family against sickness, accidents, unemployment, death
> - The promotion of equal opportunities
>   public expenditures in the areas of education, vocational training, transport, culture, leisure
>   positive discrimination measures in favor of less-privileged areas and high-risk social groups and minorities

contract and the welfare state system had become the subject of growing criticism. The welfare state has been cited for being the source of costly and inefficient bureaucratization of economic life and for creating limits to free enterprise. The adverse effects have been underscored in terms of social inequalities and new forms of social exclusion.

The dismantling of the welfare state has been most advanced in the United Kingdom and it has profoundly modified the social landscape of Western Europe. The scope of the dismantling was kept within limits until recently in Germany, the Netherlands, and the Scandinavian countries. The pressure to expand the process is, however, so strong that the remaining resistance to change has receded even in Germany and the Netherlands.[43] Germany's new ten-year program (adopted in August 1993) designed to ensure the country's future competitiveness represents a clear choice in favor of dismantling the welfare state.[44] It is centered on measures taken elsewhere in line with the trend toward privatization, deregulation, and liberalization—namely, reduction of public expenditure, in particular social security; financial, fiscal, and other regulatory incentives to promote private investments; reduction of income taxes and corporate profit taxes; stabilization and reduction of wages; further privatization of telecommunications; reduction of the role of trade unions; and the relaxation of environmental regulations that could impinge on the competitiveness of German firms. The same applies to the strong measures approved by the Dutch government at the end of November 1993.[45]

The welfare-state changes in Japan have taken the form of a slowdown or a stoppage of the building process of the modern, Western-type social contract and welfare state that began after World War II and in the 1970s in the rest of the South Asian countries. Mutatis mutandis, the same applies to Latin America. Timidly introduced after World War II, the scope and maintenance of the welfare state have been significantly reduced and threatened since the 1970s in connection with, among other things, the so-called structural adjustment policies and economic conditionality required by the International Monetary Fund and the World Bank as prerequisites for Latin American countries having access to their programs.[46]

The consequences for many countries are:

- full employment policies have been abandoned; rights to unemployment allowance have been reduced;
- financial resources in favor of the fight against poverty have been cut; coping with growing poverty in industrialized countries is increasingly left to the goodwill of the voluntary sector;
- the level of social security continues to be reduced;
- the resources allocated to the promotion of equal opportunity have vanished.

Why has this happened? Why have all industrially advanced societies, to a greater or lesser extent, turned the page on the history of the modern social contract and the welfare state? Independent of the many country-specific reasons that have influenced the pace and intensity of the destabilization and dismantling of the social contract, the main causes can be grouped in five principal categories:

- the economic crisis that began around the end of the 1960s. This favored the growth of the logic of self-interest for survival and enhanced the aggressive forms of economic competitiveness;

- the technological revolution that has transformed the manufacturing system, making millions of jobs redundant and resulting in the redesign of the sectoral and territorial landscape of industry throughout the world;
- the emerging competitive globalization of financial and other markets, production, firms' strategies and organization, shareholding;
- changes in the social structure (decline of the working class, weakness of the middle class, aging of the population) that have contributed to the resurgence of individualist and utilitarian values;
- deficits, fiscal constraints, and choices in public finance.

These combined factors have made the imperative of competitiveness the main economic and political aim of most countries. In the minds of the majority of national leaders throughout the world, especially in the most-developed countries, the maintenance of the welfare state has been equated with the loss of economic competitiveness. Today public opinion is convinced that a greater competitiveness of each country's economy is almost incompatible with the preservation of the welfare state. To give an example, according to H. Kriwet, chairman of Thyssen AG—Germany's number-one steelmaker—Germany's social net is becoming a noose around its industry. He frets that the country's industrial prowess is being eroded by welfare benefits.[47] Social justice and competitive economic success are considered irreconcilable objectives.

At the core of the dismantling process is the conviction that the more labor costs are cut and related social benefits are reduced, the better will be the country's competitiveness and effectiveness in fighting unemployment. Hence wage reductions have been demanded and imposed everywhere, and labor legislation has been weakened or negotiated away—all in the name of competitiveness. A recent report from the OECD, however, states that "low labour standards do not have much influence on external competitiveness and trade performance." Nor could poor labor market standards be shown to promote growth, job generation, or higher living standards.[48] Employment growth, the report says, is not a question of deregulation and lax labor standards. It depends "decisively on organisation and institutional structures" that sustain jobs. Figure 1.6 indicates that the United Kingdom has the lowest OECD labor standards index (that is, equal to zero), but does not perform on income level as well as Denmark, Belgium, Switzerland, Norway, Germany, and Sweden, whose labor standard indices are far higher.

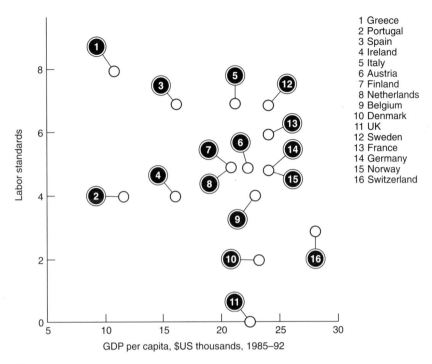

1 Greece
2 Portugal
3 Spain
4 Ireland
5 Italy
6 Austria
7 Finland
8 Netherlands
9 Belgium
10 Denmark
11 UK
12 Sweden
13 France
14 Germany
15 Norway
16 Switzerland

**Figure 1.6**
Deregulation: Not delivering the goods
Source: OECD, *Employment Outlook,* July 1994, Paris.

## The Crisis of Unemployment: The Major Social Issue of the Next Twenty Years

The data tell the story. In 1973:

• the number of unemployed in the OECD countries was 11.3 million

• of these, the share of long-term unemployed (that is, those out of work for one year or longer) was estimated on average at about one-fifth (there were marked variations among countries).

In 1991,

• the number of unemployed in the OECD countries was more than 30 million, or 6.9 percent of the active population

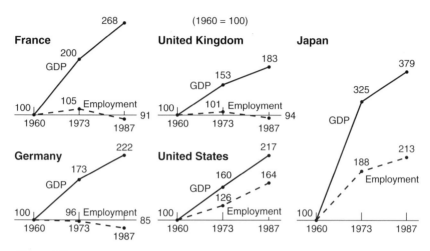

**Figure 1.7**
GDP and employment growth in industrialized countries, 1960–1987
Source: *World Human Development Report,* 1993, UNDP, New York, 1993.

● of these, the share of long-term unemployed was estimated to be almost half.[49]

According to the OECD report from which the figures above were taken, unemployment in the twenty-five countries of the OECD would reach a record 35 million in 1994, up 10 million since 1990, or 8.3 percent of the active population. Women everywhere are among the social groups most affected by unemployment and its devastating human and social effects, as they are often the first fired. Also the dismantling of the welfare state disproportionately affects women.[50]

As shown in figure 1.7, the economies of the most advanced countries did not stop growing during the period 1960–1987, but the employment rate either decreased (as was the case, for instance, in France, the United Kingdom, and Germany) or it was slower than the growth rate of GDP (for example, in the United States and Japan).

The situation in the developing countries—where full employment has never been achieved—is even worse, with the exception of the Southeast Asian countries where official statistics cite low levels of unemployment, that is, less than 3 percent. The data, it seems, largely confirm the present tendency toward a divorce between economic growth and employment. More economic growth does not necessarily or automatically mean more employment.

Why has full employment (traditionally defined in Europe as being between 1,700 and 2,000 hours per year) apparently ceased to be a realistic objective, one that no one dares any longer to propose as a priority? Should one admit that full employment was nothing more than a temporary, post–World War II phenomenon? What are the implications of the quasi-universal belief and acceptance that the economy is not able to provide a lifelong full-time job for everyone? Will this lead to a massive industrial exodus of the same magnitude as the agricultural and rural exodus, or will services activities—or new kinds of economic occupations (many people are thinking of the social economy, the informal economy)—absorb the excluded labor force? Are the reduction and sharing of working time as well as job sharing inevitable? The crisis of full employment in the richest and most industrialized countries of the world reflects, no doubt, major changes in the role of direct human labor in the production and distribution of wealth, and of employment and work in human development and social life.[51]

In a historical perspective, the substitution of direct human labor by machines in the production process seems inexorable. The wave of automation since the 1970s, associated with the new microelectronic technology and new managerial and organizational engineering—experienced especially by Japanese firms—has further accelerated the process of rationalization and job reduction in many labor-intensive sectors of the economy such as the steel industry, shipbuilding, textiles, car manufacturing, and the microelectronic component industry. The so-called lean production system, or Toyotism, which in all OECD countries is gradually replacing the old manufacturing system based on Fordism (originally developed in the United States following the introduction of Tayloristic organizational principles and the assembly line), does not deviate from this historical trend of labor substitution.[52]

Until recently, job creation in the service sector has been partly able to compensate for the decline in industrial employment,[53] just as industry compensated for the massive losses in agriculture in the first decades of this century. However, the introduction and use of automation and computer-based information processes in the service sector, which is making it ripe for the extension of a lean production system in data/images processing, will limit the role of services activities as the dam against the wave of rising unemployment. Technological breakthroughs are now occurring in all sectors of the economy, contrary to previous technological revolutions that took place in specific sectors. In the past, therefore, employment lost in one sector was gained in another. This is no longer the case today as technology is currently penetrating all sectors of the economy. A growing number of analysts and business people have serious doubts about the possibility of services activities acting as a source for job growth and, hence, ensuring a return to full employment. They anticipate that, as technology is already substituting human labor in almost all routine banking, insurance, tourism, administration, and social services, technological improvements and progress will in the future affect high value- added services, especially business services. Others still hold out great hopes that personal (family, health, elderly), community, and social services will provide an important source of job creation.[54]

The general prospects for the future however are not encouraging, if forecasts based on the assessment of the impact on jobs of so-called concurrent engineering and reengineering prove to be accurate. Concurrent engineering is a system designed to shorten overall production time by working simultaneously on different phases of production. Reengineering is a new way of improving productivity by means of several technical and human forms of reorganization of work. It encompasses the application of just-in-time inventory controls to all phases of a company's operations, thanks to the advanced and massive data-processing equipment that firms have set up over the past couple of decades. It also implies work teams, empowerment procedures, reorganization of assembly lines and offices, and outsourcing. In an article on reengineering, the *Wall Street Journal Europe* (March 19, 1993) reported that "no one has a fix on the likely political and social ramifications of re-engineering, but some estimates call for the loss of as many as 25 million American jobs, that is, between a million and 2 million American jobs each year for the next 15–20 years." The same article quotes the views of John C. Skerritt, managing partner at Andersen Consulting: "we can see many, many ways that jobs will be destroyed, but we cannot see where they will be created." Under these conditions, it is not surprising to observe that a major debate has reemerged in Western Europe and the United States on the role of technological innovation in employment growth, and on the potential solution to the crisis of full employment policy represented by a generalized reduction of working time coupled with job-sharing measures.[55]

The controversy regarding technological innovation is not about how much can and should be promoted and supported. There is no reason to resist technological innovation per se. The issue is how to balance process innovation (job saving) and product innovation (job creating), and under what conditions and for what purpose should technological innovation be promoted and diffused. If the primary goal of technological innovation is to increase competition by cost reduction, higher labor productivity, and better quality and variety of products and services, then it will not serve the objective of full employment of a country. Conversely, if technological innovation is used to enhance human competency and skills or address unsatisfied needs, then technological innovation can make a significant contribution to the maintenance and growth of employment.[56]

As to the reduction of working time and job sharing, the heart of the controversy is not whether such a solution will create new jobs, particularly since 20–25 percent of today's employment already consists of part-time jobs. The majority of European studies suggest that a gradual and diversified reduction of working time coupled with job sharing contributes to the creation of new jobs in five to ten years' time, but not enough to bring about a significant reduction in the level of unemployment. Furthermore, the conditions that have to be satisfied are so numerous that the possibility of implementing such a solution appears rather modest.[57]

Rather, the heart of the controversy is the nature, scope, pertinence, and cost-benefit relationship of the structural changes that will be necessary in the short and long term. These changes will include the whole economy, social policy, and individual and collective behaviors at the national, regional, and world levels—whatever solution is adopted to eradicate unemployment. There is a growing perception that the resolution of the crisis of employment is ultimately opening the way to an unavoidable redefinition and reconstruction of the structural elements of a new economic and social system. One must contemplate the range of possible changes to income and fiscal policy, education and training (continuing education, lifelong education, the reform of present vocational training), work organization, human resources and technological innovation (the move away from the predominant technocentric philosophy and practices), and market regulation.

What is the role of human beings and technology respectively in the production and redistribution of wealth? Could our economy and societies continue to give priority to technological innovation and to automated systems to which human resources must then adjust? Shall human labor remain a residual factor of technological capabilities? Are the French ready to share their working time with Rumanians and Senegalese? Americans and Canadians with Taiwanese and Hungarians? Japanese with Costa Ricans and Namibians? Within the context of prevailing policies, the answer is no. Since the beginning of the 1970s, technological innovation has been primarily designed and implemented with a view toward increasing the competitiveness of firms by reducing production costs, raising labor productivity, and improving the quality of goods and services. The imperative of competitiveness has led advanced economies to subordinate the role and functions of human beings to the requirements of new technologies and trade performance.

Equally, the reduction in working time and job sharing are considered to be effective instruments in increasing a firm's and country's competitiveness. The search for a higher degree of competitiveness in the world economy has been one of the main reasons for the systematic reduction in employment. Greater competitiveness, as a goal per se, has become more important than the goal of full employment.

Finally, effective answers to all of the previous questions imply new solutions to the problem of how people can productively spend less time in the labor force during their lifetime, and to the reorganization of time devoted to education (various forms of life-long education) and to retirement periods (early retirement, sabbatical periods). Though many have long advocated breaking down the tight compartments into which our lives are organized (school, work, retirement), so far only modest steps have been taken in this direction. It is, however, realistic to assume that socially equitable solutions to the employment crisis will require major structural changes in the place and role of work, changes in technology, and changes in how businesses operate in our lives in the course of the next ten to twenty years.

### The Path to Development: Westernization and Fragmentation

During the cold war, developing countries had only two paths of development open to them: either the free-market capitalist variant, and the socialist or communist command economy variant. In the 1960s, however, several attempts were made to escape from such a rigid set of alternatives. But they either failed on their own or were prevented from becoming successful. A third way (the nonalignment strategy) has not been feasible since the 1970s. The increasing visible weakness of the Eastern communist variant made the Western capitalist free-market variant the prevailing path in the 1980s for all continents. The alternative solution (that is, the delinking strategy), which was supported in the mid-1970s by a minority of intellectual and political leaders from the South, envisaged a radical disconnection from the Northern/Western system by African, Asian, and Latin American countries, but this approach failed.[54]

The International Monetary Fund and the World Bank played an important role as the financial guarantors and guardians of economic orthodoxy and stability through an instrument known as structural adjustment policies, which all underdeveloped countries were required to adopt as a condition of eligibility for loans and other financial aid.

The greater the triumph of the Western path, the more the role and effectiveness of local responses has been reduced. This has not, however, resulted in more cooperation and better-integrated initiatives and projects among the poor and the less-developed countries of the world. On the contrary, the principle and practice of competitiveness that are embodied in the Western path to development have pushed each country to seek primarily its own betterment and acceptance vis-à-vis the main Western economic players. Each less-developed country has been forced to fight against the others to attract direct investment from North America, Western Europe, and Japan. The competitive fight for survival has exacerbated the negative consequences of failures and overstated the positive long-term effects of the success stories.

Within the context of such processes, as suggested by table 1.5, the most-developed countries have often used the benefits accrued from uneven economic relations with their closer peripheries to partly finance their trade deficits with other countries. Table 1.5 shows that in 1992, European Community countries recorded trade surpluses mainly with their closer neighbors (the Canary Islands, the United Arab Emirates, Turkey, Cyprus, Lebanon, Egypt, Poland, Tunisia, Austria, Switzerland, Israel), while their trade deficits were mainly with distant countries (Japan, the United States, China, Brazil, Taiwan, South Africa, Russia, Malaysia, Thailand, South Korea). This situation has characterized to a great extent European Community trade patterns over the last ten years. This has meant that a transfer of resources—although modest—has taken place via the European Community countries, from EC peripheries in favor of the most-developed trading partners (Japan, the United States) or those newly industrialized countries (China, Brazil, Taiwan) where Community countries are increasingly investing and shifting their production activities. North America has the same pattern vis-à-vis Central and Latin America.

The overall result has been a fragmentation of the development trajectories of the poor countries of the South. This is in significant contrast to the process of growing economic integration among the most-developed countries in the context of the increasing globalization of financial markets, production, and strategies (see chapter 2). This explains, among other things, the failure of the development policies pursued in the 1980s and further justifies calling this period the lost decade. It is only recently that some poor countries have begun trying new ways of promoting schemes for regional economic cooperation (see chapter 4).

The fragmentation of the countries of the South has evolved alongside the reemergence of poverty within the rich regions of the North, while most countries of Central and Eastern Europe and the former Soviet Union have joined the group of poor and less- developed countries. The end of the cold war has made the East-West divide an empty categorization of the world. The same applies, for different reasons, to the other major divide of the world, that is, the North-South bipolarization. This division was based on an economic and social dualism (rich and poor), and, to a lesser extent, on a diversity of political systems (representative democracies versus dictatorships and single-party regimes). When the decolonization process was more or less successfully achieved on all continents in the 1960s, the development gap between North and South enabled all the countries of the third world to perceive that they shared common interests, as opposed to the common interests existing among the countries of the developed North. The North-South division was born. Some thirty years later, this division has profoundly changed in nature, and a more complex situation has emerged.

The (relative) homogeneity of the South has disappeared. A few countries from Southeast Asia have succeeded in drawing closer to the club of the industrialized countries. They are competing with the most-developed countries in almost all industrial sectors. Others (the oil monarchies from the

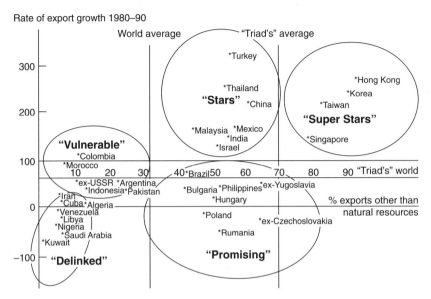

Rate of export growth 1980–90

**Figure 1.8**
A regrouping of developing countries according to their position in global trade
Source: U. Muldur, "Globalisation de la technologie et de l'économie," *CEE*, FAST, 1993, vol. 2.

Middle East) belong to the richest countries in term of GNP per capita, although their development still depends heavily on the countries of the North. Conversely, almost all African countries are victims of chronic misery and interethnic and interstate military conflicts. Different factors are at the core of a similar type of underdevelopment in Central and Indian Asia and Latin America.

There are currently at least five Souths: the newly industrialized countries of South and East Asia (the NICs); the oil-dependent South; the newly impoverished countries from the former second world of the East (that is, Rumania, Bulgaria, Poland, most of Russia, Albania, and part of the former Yugoslavia); the countries that are trying to reconvert and restructure their economic and development policies with a view toward accelerating their (re)integration into the North (Mexico, Argentina, Brazil, India, China); and, finally, the very poor South (Africa and parts of Latin America and Asia). A recent classification also gives a five-level grouping of the countries of the South (see figure 1.8).

In this figure, several oil-producing countries are defined as delinked. In fact, they are the most linked countries possible within the context of global capitalism. The figure suggests that the countries in this group are significantly losing grants, as compared to other developing countries, both in terms of export rates of growth and share of non–raw material-based exports.

The South has now disappeared as a politically united—although loose-knit—force. The third world no longer has a voice as such, and has ceased to be a strong player in global and international debates, events, and negotiations, except on environmental and human rights issues.

Of course, such profound changes do not entail the disappearance of the substantial economic and social differences and inequalities that exist in many countries and regions. The dividing line between the rich and the poor is even more pronounced than it was thirty years ago (see chapter 2). The emergence of old and new forms of poverty in the wealthy countries (44 million poor people in 1992 in the European Community, according to EUROSTAT; 8 million homeless in the United States) has meant the growth of new Souths in the North. Similarly, new Norths in the South have become very rich segments of the population, and they are often more integrated with the other Norths of the world than with the rest of their own countries.

# 2

## The New Competitive Global World

From the course of events and major changes alluded to, it is evident that the main challenge facing the world's leading social groups and countries is how to prevent the transition to a new global world from degenerating into wars of major destruction (whether military, economic, religious, or ethnic). The first section of this chapter therefore addresses important aspects of the transition, in particular the scope for action between national self-interest versus the common good, the need for identity versus the fight for survival. It concludes with a view of the present course of events: the new global world is dominated by the logic of economic warfare; it also contains the sources of major sociocultural divides of humankind that could lead to global conflicts between civilizations. The second section analyzes four specific features of the new competitive global world: the leading role played by the firm; the new alliance between the firm and the state; triadization as the present genuine form of globalization; and the process of delinking.

### Problems of Transition

#### Between Self-interest and the Common Good

In a period of transition, the directions that an individual, social group, or country may choose are numerous and not predetermined. They are not, however, infinite. The structural forces at work are the result of a combination of voluntarism, freedom, and aspirations on the one side, and adaptation, constraints, and resources on the other. Structural forces are the nonlinear shaping factors working in two directions, between the two extremes of self-interest and the global common good, as illustrated in figure 2.1.[1] Today the

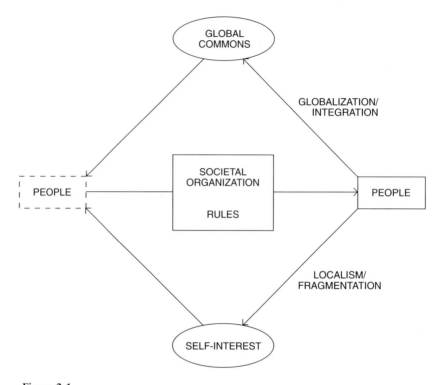

**Figure 2.1**
Between self-interest and the common good
Note: The dotted part of the figure indicates the impact on people of actual choices.

forces in favor of the line self-interest/fragmentation are very active in many regions of the world. The logic of individual survival tends, more often than not, to prevail over the logic of global coexistence and codevelopment. There is nothing new in this. However, the particularity of the present situation is that our systems of action and interaction have reached such a level of intensity that the prevailing logic of individual survival will increase the vulnerability of the whole system and may endanger the survival of humankind itself. For the first time, we are faced with the reality that global security (the logic of the global common good) is the precondition and enabling factor for individual security, and not vice-versa. This does not in any way undermine the role of the local in the global world; on the contrary, the interactions/interdependencies between the local and the global acquire a richer dimension.

Until recently, the East-West and North-South divides provided the international system with a relatively reliable basis for direction. The position of the camps was clear and stable, and each country knew to which camps it belonged. These delineations have disappeared, however, and have opened the way to an entire spectrum of choices along various lines.

The East-West divide defined the good and the bad, and everyone knew who the enemy was. Today there is no clearly identifiable enemy, and apparently everyone is good. Almost all countries share the principles and practices of the free market economy; and national capitalism is being replaced by global capitalism. A new era of international cooperation has seemingly emerged.[2] The reality, however, is rather different. Individual and collective security is perceived to be continually under threat. The North-South divide once firmly separated the rich from the poor countries; today poverty is increasing everywhere along with greater wealth disparities (the wealthiest 20 percent of the world population has become richer than it was thirty years ago, and the poorest 20 percent has grown even poorer).

The end of full-employment policies does not point to promising images for the future. Economic and social security are no longer guaranteed, and individuals are left to ensure their own survival. Competitiveness has become the overriding goal as society seems to be moving backward, especially in cities. So the question is: are the guiding principles behind the new competitive global world capable of (re)constructing the new points of reference and rules of the game that will make it easier to reach (provisional) equilibria between self-interest and the global common good and provide everyone with a sense of direction?

### The Need for Identity: The Explosion of Localism, Social Intolerance, and Exclusion

When there is either a collapse or serious destabilization of their immediate environment, people tend to look inward. The search for one's own identity becomes vital, because only this can provide a sense of direction, certainty, and stability. Knowing oneself is a central element of the human experience.

The reasons and ways to search for an identity differ considerably from one group to another. The Chinese from the thriving east coast who move dramatically fast in a capitalist type of economy—as well as those Chinese from Taiwan, who hesitate between strengthening their own state and community or joining the "Greater China"—sooner or later will need to know who they are, who they are becoming, and the direction they wish to take. Since 1992, the world press has emphasized the explosion of the capitalist economy in China. According to official statistics, the phenomenon is still insignificant: 220,000 private firms employing 3.6 million people and representing only approximately 1 percent of China's industrial capacity. This data underestimates the phenomenon and is already outdated. For the time being, the explosion of capitalism in China is largely due to the Chinese diaspora. But Western countries are exhibiting considerable interest in the potential market opportunities represented by a country where the labor cost is $60 per month lower than that in Taiwan.[3] The wave of consumerism in China has taken on such momentum that many people, including top-level leaders, are increasingly concerned about the almost entire lack of morality characterizing the overheated Chinese economy.[4] Environmental and social destruction are already evident. The gap between the newly rich elite and the masses of poor in the interior is rapidly widening. One result—combined with the 1997 deadline on Hong Kong reunification with mainland China—is a new flow of Chinese immigrants into the United States.

Similarly, the Japanese must learn to cope with an entirely new situation. Their civilization has been heavily influenced throughout history by outside civilizations: China 2,000 years ago, Europe in the sixteenth and nineteenth centuries, and the United States in this century. They have been able to react to and assimilate these foreign influences without great difficulty. Development stimulated by foreign civilizations has, however, come to an end. Japan is now considered by many to be the world's front-runner in the development of a new civilization, of which the most visible driving forces and features are associated with the technoscientific revolution—essentially the new automation, information, and communication technologies.[5] The Japanese are setting the agenda; they are exporting a new civilization of which they are codesigners and codevelopers in a context where other countries participate in both competitive and cooperative interactions. The situation is entirely new to them. It is also significantly different from their traditional process of expansion, conquest, and domination of the country by other countries. The Japanese therefore must learn the difficult task of mastering a new and unique process—new because it is the first time that they have played the leading civilian role, and because the phenomenon of leadership takes place within a context of high levels of interdependence and balanced forms of integration among the most developed societies of the world.[6] Of course, as an economic giant that has come to represent 15 percent of the world's GNP, Japan has changed considerably in the last thirty years and will continue to do so.

Not surprisingly, a major concern among Japanese intellectuals and political leaders—including those from the opposition—is to underscore the fact that Japan's only reasonable role in the international community is to strengthen the multipolar world[7] and to promote greater harmony among nations within the framework of a growing globalism.[8]

Conversely, one can easily understand the attitude of the Americans. They have been accustomed to being the world leader, particularly since World War II. After the collapse of the Soviet Union, they remain the only unchallenged military superpower. But they cannot avoid facing the fact that, in many respects, they have lost world economic and technological supremacy and cultural leadership. The United States still attracts a huge number of immigrant candidates because it offers ideals of freedom, but the United States can no longer export its way of life as the most attractive, particularly for those who are aware of the degradation of major urban centers, increasing violence, the decay of public infrastructure, the crisis in education, and the marginalization of large segments of the population. Today New York, Los Angeles, and Chicago are not regarded as model cities.

The debate is still open on the nature and scope of America's decline. Is it structural and irreversible, or relative and transitory? The relative decline is a fact.[9] This is why the leitmotif of American leaders throughout the 1980s was (and remains today under the President Clinton) "the reconquest of America's world leadership." The titles of the many books that have mirrored the domestic debate in the last ten to fifteen years are self-explanatory: *The Coming Back of America, Made in America: Regaining the Productive Edge, America Can Do It.*

"The American crisis agenda is a multifaceted one. America has lost its former self-confident monopoly over the sense of history. For the first time, the fear of being left behind or cast aside is a real one."[10] Two additional domestic factors are at work in America's crisis mentality and search for identity. First, although for the next twenty years the American demographic situation will be stable relative to that in many other parts of the world, current trends are likely to increase stress and put pressure on the American population. By the year 2000, white groups in some states (such as California and Texas) and cities will become the second largest minority, overtaken by African-Americans and especially Hispanics, who will become the most significant nonwhite group in the United States. It is difficult to say whether this will result in future years in the end of the "American ethnic dream" of social harmony despite diversity. Tensions, however, will no doubt increase.[11] The second factor is linked to America's economic, social, and urban crisis, which has resulted in the shrinking of the middle class (the traditional backbone of American development and power) and an explosion of poverty, homelessness, and violence.[12]

Americans are not alone in experiencing doubts about their society and future. European Community leaders are once again faced with growing Euroskepticism. The year 1993 was intended to usher in the new Europe, with the realization of the long glorified single market and the ratification of the treaty of the union (known as the Maastricht Treaty) by all member states. In reality the situation is quite different, particularly from a psychological and social perspective. The liberalization of internal customs (brought by the single market) that was intended to take effect on January 1, 1993, is still incomplete. People have the impression that nothing has really changed. More important, the general feeling is that the Maastricht Treaty, despite its ratification, has been politically overtaken by the "temporary" suspension of the European Monetary System. However, the economic recession is only part of the story. Many other reasons exist to explain the new wave of Euroskepticism.

First, the motivation for European integration in the 1950s (providing a bloc against the communist East; removing forever incentives for war between France and Germany; addressing the economic interests of the United States in favor of a large open European market) has lost its significance. What is the motivation, then, today? Apparently pure economic market integration does not represent a sufficient cause for mobilizing European dreams and optimism. The geographical scope is also problematic: following the collapse of the Berlin wall and the move of the central and eastern European countries toward a market economy and representative democratic system, what kind of integration should one strive for at the pan-European level? And what does Europe mean today? Is Byelorussia part of Europe? Now that in all European countries there exists a significant Muslim minority and that their integration/coexistence with Europeans will hopefully increase and improve in the next twenty to thirty years, should Turkey still be considered an impossible candidate for membership in a monetary and economic union? Finally, the people of Europe have increasing difficulty in foreseeing and planning a common development. The future remains rather ambiguous.[13]

Neither is the Arab world better positioned. Deeply divided because of power conflicts among Iraq, Syria, Jordan, Saudi Arabia, and Egypt for regional leadership, the Arab identity as well as Arab unity are, as ever, a source of persistent questioning. The Palestinian case makes a short-term and partial solution to disunity and conflicts even more problematic. The development and growth of a very active Islamic movement and militancy has not helped. On the contrary, as the case of Algeria clearly demonstrates, it has exacerbated social and political problems.[14]

The same, mutatis mutandis, applies to the Central Asian republics, where the growing influence of Islamic movements is complicating the process of establishing new politically and economically organized societies following the countries' independence from the former Soviet Union. No one can predict how the situation will evolve in the next ten to twenty years in Khazakstan, Azerbaijan, Uzbekistan, Afghanistan, or Turkistan.[15] Relations among them and with, for instance, Pakistan, Iran, India, China, and Russia, are already neither easy nor peaceful. Furthermore, the large neighboring countries of India and Russia are shaken by major internal ethnic, political, and social tensions.

The expression "identity crisis" as applied to India is less and less striking.[16] The same is not true of Russia. Identity is not the major problem for the time being; rather it is the danger of atomization of the Russian state if the request for autonomous regional status increases in the next couple of years. Evidently, in Russia the process of democratization cannot expand without excess and contradiction, particularly if one considers the extreme concentration of power and autocracy that have characterized the history both of the Soviet Union and the tsarist empire.

The quest for regional autonomy and a decentralized political system reflects a long and different history in Canada, Spain, France, and Italy.

Canada, long considered a model for the mutually enriching coexistence of its many ethnic, linguistic, religious, and regionally based groups, no longer seems capable of adapting its political structures to accommodate the natural aspirations of both the Quebecois and the "first nations." Never having fully completed its transition to a fully integrated nation-state, Canada has yet to find a formula that will satisfy the statist aspirations of its aboriginal nations, the national aspirations of its French-speaking citizens, concentrated in Quebec, and the regional forces of a country as wide as a continent. Nevertheless, the mere fact that the Canada-Quebec debate is being carried out in a civilized manner while those who advocate sovereignty for Quebec do so in a most democratic manner is encouraging for the worldwide process of political recomposition.

The success of the local leagues in Italy provides another example of the search for identity and the inability of the nation-state to provide adequate solutions. Their success, however, is not due to a struggle for more advanced forms of political democracy and stronger social cohesion and solidarity. Rather it is due to the populist response they offer to political and economic problems. They have succeeded because their analysis of the Italian situation has convinced a large segment of the middle class and the "excluded" (unemployed) that "the others" (that is, foreigners, immigrants, and those whom they term "social parasites") are the principal cause of their difficulties.[17] Similar ideas and patterns of behavior have spread throughout other countries in the last ten to fifteen years and are sustaining the explosion of xenophobia and racism once again in Germany, the United Kingdom, France, Belgium, Spain, Hungary, Slovakia, and even Sweden. Hence we bear witness to the passive and fatalist, though incredulous, reaction of European societies to the ethnic purification pursued by the Serbians and Croatians, as well as the passivity of the international community in the face of massive genocide in Rwanda and huge civilian population losses in Sri Lanka, Peru, Uganda, Ethiopia, and Pakistan, to mention merely those countries that have had the very sad privilege of being at the center of recent attention of the world mass media.

**The Imperative for Survival: Between Wars and Technocratic Illusions**
The very rapid and incomplete overview of so many different situations, connected to each other within the context of both growing interdependence and divisiveness,[18] suggests that the majority of people in the world must live

with a permanent sense of insecurity. The promotion and defense of one's own identity is accompanied by the rejection or destruction of another's. Uncertainty creates greater uncertainty, and more hostility breeds more violence. Many human beings are prisoners of the logic of war, fighting against others in order to guarantee their own survival. The "other" is almost unanimously and automatically suspected of being an enemy, a potential source of danger—at least a challenge to one's existence and identity.

In most cases, war is the extreme remedy when the tensions accumulated in the fight for survival have reached the highest level. In some other cases, it is also the easiest option, particularly for groups in power who have demonstrated their inability to cope with tensions and difficulties in a constructive manner. Beside military conflicts and social intolerance and exclusion, another way of coping with the imperative of survival that is being increasingly adopted at the country level is technological innovation and development. The mastery of the most advanced and cheapest technology, which enables the selling of products and services in the most profitable and promising markets, is increasingly used as the instrument to ensure survival. Salvation—people are informed—lies in technology. Competitive technological innovation in global markets (preferably privatized, deregulated, and liberalized markets) imposes itself as the only effective regulator of the dynamic of the fight for survival. Technical progress has always been a primary source of economic development. In contemporary societies, however, technology has acquired unparalleled functions.

Be it the way we design and produce goods and services (automation, robots, artificial intelligence); manage plants, animals, and our own bodies (drugs, genetic engineering, scanners, noninvasive therapy); build roads, tunnels, cities, and houses (new materials, telematics, fiber optics); use leisure time (mass media, electronic appliances, modes of transport); or the way we express individual and collective artistic creativity (image processing, computer art, virtual reality), no human activity seems free from the pervasive influence of technology.[19] Our language bears witness to this: we talk about computer illiteracy, the information superhighway, intelligent houses, self-reproducible robots, test-tube babies. In line with his vision of technology as "an engine for economic growth," President Clinton has clearly made strengthening U.S. technological innovation capabilities nothing less than a national priority, saying, "Leadership in developing and commercializing new technologies is critical to rejoining industrial leadership, creating high-wage jobs and ensuring our long-term prosperity." The strategic relevance of technology for society and the dependence of the country's well-being on technology could not be better underscored.

The "technologization" of society is not a new phenomenon. It began when humankind invented and used its first external tools (a stone, for example) and related techniques (rules governing the production and the use of the tools). The novelty lies in the nature and scope of the intensification and extensification processes of the rise of technology in society in the last half century. These processes reflect fundamental breakthroughs in basic knowledge and related technology concerning the four pillars of organized human society: energy, materials, living organisms, and information.

Forty years ago, genetic engineering such as medically assisted procreation or biologically modified organisms were concepts and processes that existed only in the fertile minds of scientists and science-fiction writers. Today they are on the agenda of public debates in almost all advanced countries where these ideas are now being developed and applied. The new biotechnologies may raise the productivity of existing plants and animals; enable a better and safer selection of plants; design and produce new drugs; and facilitate the use of microorganisms for environmental purposes (urban waste treatment, for instance).[20] Their development and use, however, raise a series of fundamental ethical and social questions that are still unresolved.

Should one, for example, authorize the commercial patenting of microorganisms? Not all countries have made a decision. Some, like the United States, have given a positive response. Others are very reluctant to move in this direction because of the possible adverse effects associated with commercial patenting. Within what limits can the emission of biologically modified organisms into the environment be authorized? Who decides the conditions and controls under which medically assisted procreation (that is, gene transplant or gene modification) can be authorized? How can one be sure that the purpose of the intervention will remain a genetic therapy and not a deliberate form of eugenics? In the United States, the use of genetic code identification has been authorized in criminal testing. Should insurance companies and other enterprises also be permitted to use it before an insurance or employment contract is signed?[21] By nature, the majority of chemical and pharmaceutical firms and other health-related industries—to give but a few examples—strongly favor the free development and use of this new technology. Their primary motivation is, of course, economic. They see the enormous potential for market opportunities and development. Technologists also tend to influence public decisionmakers in favor of the adoption of more permissive rules and approaches. In their view, these processes are the source of major technological revolutions that will contribute to the greater well-being of humankind. The reality is much more complex, as illustrated by the results of several technological assessment exercises undertaken in Denmark, Sweden, France, Germany, the United States, and Japan.[22] Commercial, economic, and market aspects cannot prevail over social, political, and ethical issues and choices.

Vast new opportunities have also been opened up by progress made in the energy field. Outside the still highly controversial role for civilian uses of nuclear energy, which represents one of the major historical breakthroughs in science and technology ever accomplished by human beings, energy-saving technology as well as technology designed for the exploitation of renewable energy sources have contributed to the modification of the energy landscape, especially in the most industrialized countries.[23] Here again, the opportunities made possible have produced several negative consequences and created a variety of major problems and challenges (particularly of an environmental nature, not to mention urban congestion and ways of life that waste resources).[24]

The same applies to the other family of technology, that is, information and communication technologies (hereafter IT). Even more than energy technology and biotechnology, IT are considered the principal source of the "third industrial revolution" that began with the microelectronics revolution in the 1960s. Many new terms hype this revolution: information society, computer society, computer revolution, paperless society, information economy, informediation society, information technology paradigm. It is not necessary to agree or disagree with such popular views; the reality is that information and communication technologies have had a major impact, for better or worse,[25] on all key economic activities—their nature (more and more dematerialized), their organization at the factory and office level, and their territorial distribution/concentration, both within and across countries. IT have a structural influence on work organization and work conditions,[26] the expansion and transformation of services activities, the relations between private firms and public authorities, and the linkages between small and medium-sized enterprises (SMEs) and large firms. They have been one of the primary sources of the explosion and globalization of financial and business services. Information and communication technologies have redesigned firms' and countries' comparative advantages.[27] They have contributed to increasing the concentration of access to information and decisionmaking, control and power. As the key factor in furthering labor-substitution processes in manufacturing as well as in service activities, they have accelerated the crisis of full employment.[28] They have, in general, contributed to the intensification of competitiveness both in economic and social affairs.

Because of their enormous potential for application to almost all socioeconomic areas, information and communication technologies have been considered powerful instruments for solving the many crucial problems of contemporary societies. The result is that an array of techno-utopias and technological fixes have come to dominate the scene. Thus,

- there is a widespread belief that the urban crisis will be resolved through the development of new information and communication infrastructures and services in transport, mail delivery, health and social services, tourism, leisure, teleworking, and teletraining;
- computer-based planning, monitoring, and control systems are presented as facilitators of better, cheaper, and more efficient development and management of intra- and interurban transportation;
- IT are hailed as the major new means for increasing the competitiveness of cities at the international level, as well as for developing isolated peripheral regions and rural areas;
- participatory democracy—we are told—will be facilitated by a network of information and communication systems based on instant electronic technologies.

The relatively short history (less than thirty years) of applying and extending IT invites prudence in assessing their role. One statement is nevertheless supported by wide empirical evidence: technological fixes have proved to be only a part of the story and, in most cases, not the most decisive one.[29]

## Toward New Divides: Conflicts between Civilizations?
### The Competitive Economic War
What will replace the world that is gone? What will emerge from the present changes? There is a risk that new divisions of the world will emerge or will

be imposed by political and cultural forces based on the identification of new enemies. Furthermore, the analysis of the transition problems has shown that the temptation is growing everywhere to replace the old world by technocratic illusions. According to some, the new world will emerge as a result of a long period of cultural conflict among individuals and countries.[30] This argument is very compelling; it is based on the observation that different cultural identities and civilizations are not only a basic product of centuries of human history, but have also generated prolonged violent conflicts. It underlines the fact that most of the present political, economic, and military conflicts in the world are due to ethnic, religious, and cultural clashes. It also suggests that although the world is shrinking (that is, the interactions among people of different civilizations are increasing, and hence there is a growing potential for cooperation, but even more for hostility) and the Western system has become the dominant reference system, non-Western civilizations are moving toward introspection. This reaction takes various names: "re-Islamicization of the Middle East," "Hinduization" of India, "Asianization" of Japan, and so on.

Thus, "the most important conflicts of the future will occur along the cultural fault lines separating civilizations.[31] The clash of civilizations is occurring and will continue to occur at two levels. At the micro level, adjacent groups along the fault lines between civilizations struggle, often violently, for the control of territory and each other. At the macro level, states from different civilizations compete for relative military and economic power, struggle over the control of international institutions and third parties, and competitively promote their particular political and religious values. The clashes between civilizations are replacing the political and ideological boundaries of the cold war as the flashpoints for crisis and bloodshed."[32] Accordingly, some predict a future characterized by:

- the West's next confrontation coming from the Muslim world, reflecting "the peoples' irrational but surely historic reaction of an ancient rival against our Judeo-Christian heritage, our similar present, and the worldwide expansion of both;"[33]
- new major clashes between Slavs and Turks and between Muslims and Hindus on the Indian subcontinent;
- the increase of "ethnic cleansing" operations;
- and, last but not least, the possibility that "the next world war, if there is one, will be a war between civilizations."[34]

These propositions deserve to be treated with great caution, all the more so because an important bias underlies them: the author suggests that the war between civilizations will be a war between "the West and the rest."[35] Hence the practical recommendation most frequently derived from this analysis is that the West must prepare itself to deal with such a possibility.[36] Very rarely is the operational conclusion that the West (and the rest) should strive to establish the positive, cooperative mechanisms and institutions that will make it possible to eliminate, or at least reduce, the major sources of conflict.

Conversely, an interesting analysis is offered by Benjamin R. Barber, who suggests that both the tendency toward one homogenized technocratic world (which he calls "the McWorld globalization") and the opposing tendency toward the resurgence of ethnic/religious tribalism (in his terminology, "the jihad") are threatening democracy and preventing the individual citizen (as opposed to the individual customer and the individual follower) from playing a socially constructive role.[37] Stressing the fallacies behind the feigned rationality of the global technocracy and of cultural and religious integralism, the author argues that democracy will be preserved and expanded in the future via regional confederations based on socioeconomic and cultural entities smaller than nation-states. Present attempts to create regional economic and political unions are a step in this direction.

What emerges more clearly and strongly, however, is a new global world characterized, for the time being, by a new type of war: the competitive technoeconomic war for global leadership. Based on the current tendencies and key strategies of the most powerful players, the competitive technoeconomic war will be the strongest driving force and dividing line of world development and politics for the next fifteen to twenty years, if present policies continue to influence individuals', groups', and countries' visions, choices, and actions.

## Features of the New Competitive Global World

The globalizing firm seems to be among the few organizations that is able to adjust to the new global world marked by the competitive technoeconomic war for global leadership.

## The Firm: The Number One Global Actor

Contrary to internationalization—in the context of which the nation-state maintained its basic role of reference space and source of power—globalization is further extending the process initiated by multinationalization, that is, the emergence of the global firm as the key actor in the economy and society. It is increasingly recognized that the global firm is replacing public authorities as the leading actor in directing and controlling the world economy. National economic authorities hold enormous decisionmaking power in economic affairs through monetary and fiscal policies, trade regulation, provision of public services, public procurement markets, public works, and norms and standards. Their power, however, has been considerably reduced by twenty years of intensive and systematic measures of privatization, deregulation, and liberalization which, conversely, have increased the economic power of private firms and private-based mechanisms and rules. Furthermore, globalization processes have contributed to the germination and diffusion of the idea that the power of national public authorities is largely negative, that is, an obstacle to the fully free functioning of the market economy at both the international and global levels. The nation-state's action has been presented as source of constraint and not of opportunity.

The situation is entirely different with regard to private firms. The large multinational corporations have successfully recovered from the crisis of trust and credibility that affected them in the 1960s and the beginning of the 1970s. They are now regarded with great respect and confidence and are being courted by all. Why? There are several reasons.

First, firms have proved to be sufficiently flexible in adapting to changing conditions, particularly to the new globalization process. Going global has been far easier for firms than for governments, parliaments, trade unions, or universities. This is what Philippe de Woot has called the strategic capability of firms for innovation and adaptation of their attitudes and behavior to the changing context.[38]

Because of the greater difficulties faced by other actors, firms have found themselves alone as the real global players. The process of multinationalization has paved the way for the transformation and adaptation of the firm. The second reason is linked to the fact that our societies have given increasing importance these last forty years to the imperative of growth and the production of more and more goods. Fascinated by the remarkable progress of our technology, we have set at the top of our priorities the "culture of objects."

Hence the dominant culture is one that is determined and shaped by firms. As producers of the objects, technology infrastructures, and services that are shaping the new world economy, firms tend to claim that what is good for the firm is good for the world.

A third explanation exists supporting the position of the firm as the key actor. According to the investigation of the former United Nations Center on Transnational Corporations, one-third of world trade in 1991 was accounted for by intracompany transactions. Consequently, world trade statistics based on commercial flows among countries have become increasingly inadequate to understand the changing features of world trade. Thus, traditional international trade analysis loses part of its foundation and reliability when based simply on a country's comparative advantage. The same applies to the assessment of country's international competitiveness based on differences in trade performance. To think of the world economy as a system of free exchanges of flows is becoming unrealistic: the intersubsidiary transactions of firms respond to an entirely different logic than that of free trade.

The fourth reason is that most of the factors and processes that determine the economic development of a country—such as the level of employment—operate increasingly on a scale that renders national governments and institutions unable to control them. The global networks of multinational firms, on the contrary, are considered able to control them and, therefore, are the actors on which the economic and social well-being of a country is increasingly dependent. Accordingly, a new alliance between the firm and the state has been established.[39]

### The New Alliance between the Firm and the State

The new relationships between the firm and the state and between economic and political power are some of the most significant features of present processes of globalization. At first glance, these new relationships appear to be emerging in two ways. First, the most significant decisions, which relate to the allocation of technological and economic resources (those that change the present and shape the future) and which concern several countries and regions of the world, are taken mainly by large global companies (Olivetti, Alcatel, IBM, Mitsubishi, Nestlé, Thomson, Siemens, BP, BASF, Monsanto, Ericsson, Northern Telecom, Nissan, Société Générale). Especially in recent years, when instances of industrial restructuring have followed one after another and takeover bids—even gigantic ones (up to $24 billion)—have continued to make the headlines, it seems that enterprises recast the world as they deem fit (through systems involving telecommunications, large-scale distribution, agribusinesses, car manufacturers, insurance companies, etc.). This power is extended to domains that have previously escaped business influence, such as universities. Second, the state seems to be playing an increasingly less important role compared to that of the enterprise. States seem to react rather than anticipate, follow rather than lead.

Neither of these two points does full justice to a reality that is more complex and subtle. The new reality is not to be found at this level. The question is not whether enterprises are running the show, with states merely playing follow-the-leader and acting like clerks of the court, recording decisions taken by others. The new phenomenon is that owing, inter alia, to globalization, states and enterprises have entered into a new dynamic alliance. The state is not being led. It is still active—indeed, increasingly active in the world's technological and economic spheres. But it does not act as a leader.

In an awkward sense, the firm is in the process of becoming the main organization "governing" the world economy, with the support of local states as small as Denmark or as large as the United States. According to this view, the state acts as a willing accomplice, aware of its role. There is no conspiracy against the state. Because it realizes that, within the dynamics of advancing globalization of the economy, its role is bound to change radically in the long term, the state is currently assuming as its historical function the task of ensuring that its own key strategic actors—that is, the local multinationals (the only ones suited and armed to act within the world economy)—should succeed in carrying out the globalization of the national economy. The underlying argument is as follows: the success of the national enterprises on the world scene is a prerequisite for the achievement and preservation of the country's technological and economic autonomy.

This logic reflects a whole series of conditions and objective forces expressed by the following factors:

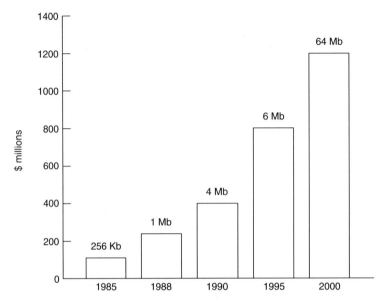

**Figure 2.2**
R&D costs for units of DRAM memory (millions of dollars)
Source: *Le Temps des Affaires,* Geneva, no. 48, October 1992.

• Growth of integration between technologies (data processing and tele-communications, microelectronics, composite materials, and optical tech-nologies) and sectors (agriculture, chemistry and energy, remote data processing, and mass media). This forces enterprises to look for ways to cover—either directly or indirectly—all sectors likely to affect the future development of their specific field of activity. In this context, an alliance with the state in countries that count is important to ensure that those sectors are well covered.

• The cost of R&D is rising. More than $3 billion is needed to design and develop a new generation of megacarriers such as Boeing 777s; the devel-opment of a new conversion system of digital telephones will also cost nearly $3 billion; inventing and developing a simple new industrial enzyme costs approximately $100 million. (Figure 2.2 shows costs associated with the development of computer memory.) These rising costs, against a background of uncertainty, force enterprises to seek help from other enterprises (often foreign) and from the state.

• Shorter product life cycles (six to eight months in the clothing trade; two or three years in automation and data processing) require high rates of depreciation and very large markets. Consequently, access to several public contracts becomes a major strategic aim.

A relative scarcity of highly qualified personnel exists in the most advanced industrialized countries. This forces enterprises to seek what they need anywhere they can find it, and the state to invest in R&D programs and universities to guarantee the highly advanced training required by enterprises. In this situation, enterprises must seek out alliances that result in systematic and close cooperation agreements with other enterprises, even rivals, in a wide range of sectors in various countries. The explosion of cooperative agreements in all economic sectors to which we have previously referred, in particular the high-technology sectors (microelectronics, robotics, telecommunications, aerospace, biotechnology), bears witness to a new form of enterprise behavior: cooperation among enterprises becomes an instrument for remaining or becoming competitive in the world economy.

Business increases its performance and its competitiveness when it integrates itself into a cumulative process of development in which it is simultaneously the driving force (the subject) and the result (the object). This process is larger than the business alone, since it includes the commercial, technological, and political environments that have a decisive influence on a business's chances of success. Yet the process itself is also strongly influenced by the business, which, by seizing opportunities and constantly readjusting the competitive stakes through its strategic initiatives, is a driving—and often innovative—force.

Such a process creates an atmosphere of competitiveness. For large businesses, it is based on the following elements:

- long-term perspectives and the existence of extensive opportunities to justify the risk involved in new technological developments and large-scale investments; these perspectives can be brought into being by large open markets, rapidly growing demand, and large-scale public projects;
- the creation by the business of sufficient strategic capacity to enable it to act on a global scale in key sectors;
- the acquisition of competitive advantages on an international scale, arising from increased strategic capacity;
- sufficient profitability to cover the costs of globalization, as well as the risks inherent in such a strategy.

Thus, one observes the same enterprises involved in several networks of cooperation and alliances with various partners which, in the final analysis, are interlocked around more or less easily definable clusters of technologies, products, and markets.[40] The overall emerging pattern is one of a series of oligopolistic world structures, creating the danger of cartels.

The main features and structures of a large number of enterprises and industrial sectors are in a process of thorough transformation. For example, in 1980, thirteen companies shared 80 percent of world turnover in the tire industry. In 1990 no more than six companies produced 85 percent of the total output, and many experts and industrialists feel that between now and the year 2000 there may be only three or four large firms monopolizing the world tire industry, perhaps in the form of a cartel.[41]

To globalize effectively, enterprises are also forced to seek maximum support from their own state. This may actually mean support from several states, owing to the enterprises' location in more than one country, and to the role they play in the national economies of those countries. Thus despite their general rhetoric in calling for "less state and more market," enterprises expect the state to keep them covered in the rearguard (that is, to secure markets for their established products) as well as in the vanguard (that is, to assure them a place in the development of new products). In fact, enterprises require four categories of support and service from the state:

• Covering the costs of basic infrastructures (funding basic and high-risk research; funding universities and vocational training systems; promoting and funding mechanisms for the dissemination of scientific and technical information and technology transfers);

• Providing the tax incentives needed for investment in industrial R&D and technological innovations;

• Guaranteeing that enterprises from the given country (national enterprises) should have a sufficiently stable industrial base with privileged access to the internal market via public contracts (defense, telecommunications, health, transport, education, social services). Public contracts, particularly those in high-technology strategic sectors (defense, telecommunications, data processing), also play a twofold major role: acquiring and financing a certain degree of basic scientific and technical competence for the enterprises; and protecting a certain sector of the internal market on which local enterprises may depend;

• Providing the necessary support and assistance (regulatory, commercial, diplomatic, political) to local enterprises in their activities and their fight for survival on external markets.

Enterprises also require from the state legislation and policies favorable to their freedom of action (in particular in the field of labor market regulation). In exchange for this support, the enterprises guarantee the state that they will remain or become competitive in world markets and, thanks to their enhanced innovative capacity, they promise in this way to contribute to the nation's technological independence, to produce and provide wealth for the country, and thus help create jobs. In turn, the state has an objective, direct, and immediate interest in supporting local enterprises. Indeed, since national independence and economic well-being depend ever more on the mastery and marketing of advanced basic technologies (semiconductors, composite materials, robotics, highly sophisticated instrumentation, microcomputing, supercomputers, cognitive sciences, biological technologies), the state is increasingly dependent on the innovation capability and control of world markets that the enterprises ensure. The state's political and social legitimacy, which is based on its ability to secure the country's continuous socioeconomic development, is at issue. The state therefore has every interest in intervening in support of its own national enterprises. It does so by mapping out and pursuing a technological, industrial, and commercial policy whose form differs from country to country, but which—within the framework of the OECD—obeys the same logic and is inspired by the same principle: to mobilize the available national resources in the service of short- and medium-term commercial success on world markets by the national enterprises (small- and medium-sized businesses and large multinational companies), especially the best, the strongest, the winners among them.

Thus despite some distinct nation-specific features, most states are adopting the same strategy: by means of national R&D programs and participation in public international programs, manipulation of public markets, tax breaks, and commercial measures, they carry out a massive transfer of collective public resources to private enterprises, mostly multinational corporations, to enable them to remain competitive in the so-called fight for survival at the world level. In so doing, all states hope to ensure the conditions needed for the economic development of the country and thus protect the basis of their legitimacy. In other words, states tend to maintain their own social role by delegating de facto to the enterprises the task of ensuring the socioeconomic development of the country.

Such is the nature of the new alliance: enterprises need local (national) states to cope with globalization and to globalize themselves. The states need global enterprises to ensure the continuity of their legitimacy and perpetuation as local political and social entities. Accordingly, the enterprises gradually acquire historical legitimacy and a social role that in many respects approximates the legitimacy and role appropriate to the state. As a result, on a world scale there is increasing separation of economic and political power.

The more a company becomes globalized, the more it is likely to lose its own identity within a tangle of companies, alliances, and markets. In this process maintaining and expanding its own decisionmaking power and its ability to control the allocation of the planet's material and nonmaterial resources to which the enterprise may, and hopes to, have access, become the only true objectives. An enterprise knows, however, that if it restricted itself to just these goals it would sooner or later be swept off the economic map by stronger enterprises allied with the stronger states. It therefore needs to acquire a social legitimacy in the eyes of both local society (the country) and world society. The alliance with the state enables it to find the new legitimacy it needs. Through the alliance it may claim that the state has assigned it the task of defending and promoting the economic and social well-being of the local society, by ensuring its own industrial and commercial success on the world scene—a claim the state cannot deny. As far as global society is concerned, the enterprise lays claim to a kind of legitimacy based on the fact that it has become globalized. It makes this claim implicitly in that it presents itself as the only organization able to assure the optimal worldwide management of available material and nonmaterial resources. De facto, therefore, the enterprise privatizes (and internationalizes for its own purposes) the role of the state. It does so repeatedly in all the countries where it is active and where it can claim to form an integral part of the local country and be a determining factor in the economic and social well-being of this country. Similarly—in the absence of a world public governance—it privatizes more and more the function of organizing and governing the world economy.

## Triadization

The privatization of the function of organizing and governing the world economy is not inconsistent with another key characteristic of present globalization processes. Today's globalization is a truncated globalization. "Triadization" is a more correct term for the current situation.[42] Triadization means that the process of technological, economic, and sociocultural integration among the three most developed regions of the world (Japan plus the NICs from South and Southeast Asia, Western Europe, and North America) is more diffuse, intensive, and significant than integration between these three regions and the less-developed countries, or between the less-developed countries themselves.

Triadization also exists in peoples' minds. According to the Japanese, the North Americans, and the West Europeans, the world that counts is their world where cultural and scientific power, technological supremacy, military hegemony, and economic wealth are all located and, therefore, so is the ability to govern the world economy and society and to shape its future.

The phenomenon of triadization is demonstrated in the geographical patterns of interfirm alliances. Of the 4,200 interfirm strategic cooperation agreements signed by enterprises worldwide in the period 1980–1989, 92 percent were between enterprises from Japan, Western Europe, and North America (see table 2.1, column 3). Available statistics on foreign direct investments also reveal that in the last ten years Japan, the United States, and Western Europe have invested increasingly among themselves. The triadization of FDI is the result of investment flows that have created a fundamentally different international economic situation from that of the 1960s and 1970s. Until the beginning of the 1980s, the developing countries had a role to play, albeit a limited one, as countries of origin and of destination. During the 1980s, the triad accounted for around four-fifths of all international capital flows. The developing countries' share fell from 25 percent to 19 percent in the 1970s—despite a 30 percent rate of growth per year in FDI and a near doubling of average annual flows to the developing countries between 1980–1984 and 1985–1989.[43] Although the flow of foreign direct investments destined for Latin America, Asia (NICs excluded), or even Africa may increase again, the tendency will remain as one of preference directed toward the regions of the triad. The same trend applies to the other two components of capital flows, together with foreign direct investments,

**Table 2.1**
Distribution of interfirm strategic technology alliances
by field and group of countries, 1980–1989

| Fields of technology | Number of alliances (1) | % for developed economies (2) | % for triad (3) | % for triad-NIC (4) | % for triad-LDC (5) | Other (6) |
|---|---|---|---|---|---|---|
| Biotech. | 846 | 99.1 | 94.1 | 0.4 | 0.1 | 0.5 |
| New materials | 430 | 96.5 | 93.5 | 2.3 | 1.2 | — |
| Computer | 199 | 98.0 | 96.0 | 1.5 | 0.5 | — |
| Industrial automation | 281 | 96.1 | 95.0 | 2.1 | 1.8 | — |
| Microel. | 387 | 95.9 | 95.1 | 3.6 | — | 0.5 |
| Software | 346 | 99.1 | 96.2 | 0.6 | 0.3 | — |
| Telecom. | 368 | 97.5 | 92.1 | 1.6 | 0.3 | 0.5 |
| Misc. IT | 148 | 93.3 | 92.6 | 5.4 | 0.7 | 0.7 |
| Automot. | 205 | 84.9 | 82.9 | 9.8 | 5.4 | — |
| Aviation | 228 | 96.9 | 94.3 | 0.9 | 1.3 | 0.9 |
| Chemical | 410 | 87.6 | 80.0 | 3.9 | 7.1 | 1.5 |
| Food & beverages | 42 | 90.5 | 76.2 | 9.5 | — | — |
| Heavy electr. | 141 | 96.5 | 92.2 | 1.4 | 2.1 | — |
| Instr. | 95 | 100.0 | 100.0 | — | — | — |
| Others | 66 | 90.9 | 77.3 | 1.5 | 4.5 | 3.0 |
| Total | 4192 | 95.7 | 91.9 | 2.3 | 1.5 | 0.5 |

Source: Chris Freeman and John Hagedoorn, *Globalization of Technology*, Report for the FAST Program, Commission of the European Communities, June 1992, p. 41.

namely, monetary and financial flows (we have shown the triadization process in figures 1.3 and 1.4) and portfolio investments and other types of financial transactions. The triadic countries are increasingly interacting and integrating with each other.

## Delinking

If the target is to win, only a few will succeed. The losers will be excluded and abandoned to their situation. The winners will continue to remain together, and increasingly integrate with one other. The need for maintaining or reestablishing linkages between the excluded and the integrated declines in importance. Thus a new divide in the world appears, coinciding with the emergence of globalization. Delinking is the process through which some countries and regions are gradually losing their connections with the most economically developed and growing countries and regions of the world. Rather than participating in the processes of increasing interconnections and integration that are constructing the new global world, they are moving in the opposite direction. Delinking affects almost all countries of Africa, most parts of Latin America and Asia (with the exception of countries from Southeast Asia), as well as parts of the former Soviet Union and Eastern Europe.

The available data is self-explanatory. In 1980 the share of world trade of manufactured goods of the 102 poorest countries of the world was 7.9 percent of world exports and 9 percent of imports. Just ten years later, these shares fell to 1.4 percent and 4.9 percent respectively (see table 2.2). Conversely, the share of the three regions of the triad increased from 54.8 percent to 64.0 percent of world exports and from 59.5 percent to 63.8 percent of world imports.

**Table 2.2**
Relative share of the world market for manufactured goods

|  | Exports | | Imports | |
|---|---|---|---|---|
|  | 1980 | 1990 | 1980 | 1990 |
| Industrialized world (24 countries) | 62.9 | 72.4 | 67.9 | 72.1 |
| of which G7 (USA, CND, J, D, F, UK, I) | 45.2 | 51.8 | 48.2 | 51.9 |
| ● the triad | 54.8 | 64.0 | 59.5 | 63.8 |
| ● other industrialized countries | 8.1 | 8.5 | 8.4 | 8.3 |
| Developing world (148 countries) | 37.1 | 27.6 | 32.1 | 27.9 |
| of which, |  |  |  |  |
| group "stars" (11 countries) | 7.3 | 14.6 | 8.8 | 13.5 |
| group 1: the poorest (102 countries) | 7.9 | 1.4 | 9.0 | 4.9 |
| Total | 100 | 100 | 100 | 100 |

Source: Ugur Muldur, *Les formes et les indicateurs de la globalization*, FAST, Commission of the European Communities, 1993.

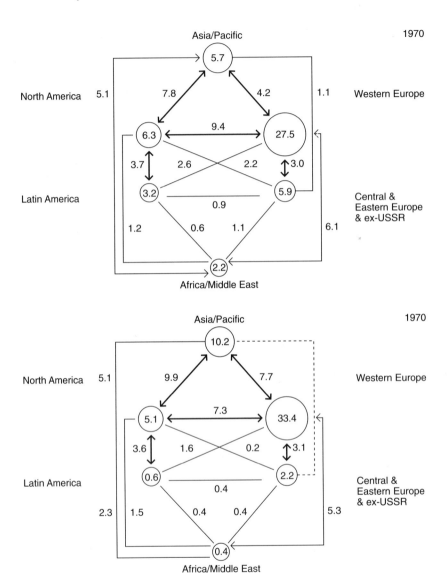

**Figure 2.3**
Share of regional trade flows of world trade of manufactured goods (in percent of total world trade), 1970 and 1990

Source: Ugur Muldur, *Les formes et les indicateurs de la globalisation*, FAST, Commission of the European Communities, Brussels, 1993.

Further evidence is found in that in 1970 intracontinental exchanges within each of the three regions of North America, Western Europe, and Pacific/Asia, represented 21.4 percent of world trade of goods. If one adds intercontinental exchanges between them (39.4 percent), these regions represented 60.8 percent of world trade in 1970 (see figure 2.3).

In 1990 cumulative intracontinental exchanges within each region were 48.7 percent, and the intercontinental exchanges between the three regions rose to 24.9 percent. Altogether, the exchanges of the three regions made up 73.6 percent of world trade, the remaining 26.4 percent being shared among Russia and Central Europe, the Middle East, Africa, and Latin America.

It is worth noting the high rate of growth of intracontinental exchanges concerning Pacific/Asia and Western Europe, which moved from 6.3 percent to 10.2 percent and 27.1 percent to 33.4 percent respectively. In contrast, the intracontinental share of Africa and the Middle East fell from 14.1 percent in 1970 to 9.9 percent in 1990, that of Latin America from 7.8 percent to 6.1 percent, and that of the countries from the ex-communist bloc from 7.3 percent to 4.1 percent. In other words, the world economy has been characterized in the last twenty years, at least, by a gradual reduction of the exchanges between the richest and fast-growing countries of North America, Western Europe, and Pacific Asia and the rest of the world, Africa in particular. If this tendency were to be extrapolated for the next twenty years, the share of Africa, the Middle East, Latin America, Russia, and Central/Eastern Europe that was 39.2 percent of world trade in 1970 and 26.4 percent in 1990 would be reduced to 5 percent in 2020. That is delinking. That is the new division of the world between the increasingly integrated global world and the increasingly excluded fragments of the world.

# 3

## Can Competition Govern the Planet?

### The Critical Choice

#### Scenarios for the Next Twenty Years

The picture that emerges from the preceding chapters is fairly clear. New global processes have developed. They have been generated by new ideas, greater scientific and technological capabilities, and new aspirations. The map of the world economy and society has changed. The principles, rules, and actions centered on the nation-state and the national economy as well as on the East-West ideological cleavage of the cold war have disappeared or undergone profound transformation. New actors have emerged around the global network of multinational firms and the global civilian society.

New disorders have been created at the same time that prospects for a new global order have appeared. Our societies are in search of principles and rules for a new governance of global society, and many solutions have been proposed. We are confronted with having to chose from among three basic alternative futures: the competition for survival, pax triadica, and global governance. These three options emerge from an in-depth analysis of possible scenarios for the next twenty years. The following scenarios are based on ten major assumptions that sum up most of the issues discussed so far (see box 3.1).

1. The new processes of the globalization of research, technology, and the economy will intensify. Triadization (increasing trade and economic integration among Western Europe, North America, Japan, and Southeast Asia) will remain the prevailing form of economic globalization in the context of the increasing regionalization of economic areas (the European Community, the North American Free Trade Area, the Asian Free Trade Area, Mercosur,

**Box 3.1**
Basic assumptions

---

1. Triadization of the world economy in the context of the new processes of globalization will continue.

2. The distribution of the world population by 2020 will be increasingly unbalanced, Asia will be the dominant region economically, and Africa will be very poor.

3. The interests of the developed countries will continue to orient the global agenda of science and technology toward privatization, deregulation, and liberalization of the economy.

4. The world divide (integrated vs. excluded) will be exacerbated.

5. A new techno-organizational revolution will shape the manufacturing system and industry as a whole.

6. Large firms will increasingly become involved in networks or webs of networks. Small and medium-sized firms will be subject to massive reorganization and market processes.

7. A new, massive wave of unemployment will explode if present trends continue.

8. The "greening" of industry will expand within the constraints imposed by competitiveness.

9. Cities and city-regions will become the relevant space of the reorganization of the globalizing economy.

10. Strategies of public authorities will fluctuate between a fully fledged market economy and a tempered social market economy with moderate protectionism.

---

the Maghreb). Both industrial wars and agreements of cooperation will mark the (relatively) unstable process of triadization.

2. The world population will be closer to 7 billion people between 2010 and 2015. The European population will be 300–310 million, while the Asian population will be more than 3.5 billion, and Africa will surpass the 1 billion figure in a context of massive poverty.

3. If present trends are maintained, the global science and technology agenda will be to a significant extent designed and guided by the interests of the most developed regions and countries of the world. Priority areas will be identified in terms of their expected contributions to the industrial and economic competitiveness of local firms. R&D policy will remain an essential component of, or a surrogate to, industrial policy in the context of generalized market privatization, deregulation, and liberalization.

4. Accordingly, the tendency toward the division between those cities, regions, countries, and social groups that will remain or become members of the highly technologically developed world at the triadic level and those that will be part of the gradually marginalized and excluded world of poverty and underdevelopment will be strengthened.

5. A new techno-organizational revolution will reshape the manufacturing system, the service economy, the sectoral structures, and the firms themselves. Automation, information, and communication technology will remain the major sources of technologically led changes and increases in productivity. Greater energy and materials efficiency and productivity will enhance the changes arising from these three sources.

New processes, products, and services resulting from innovations in biotechnology will become increasingly evident and diffused in the next ten years. Lean production (Toyotism) seems to be regarded, at least for the coming ten to fifteen years, as the new model of manufacturing production to be adopted in the highly technologically advanced countries and regions. This does not mean that Fordist and neo-Fordist types of mass production will disappear. A vast process of reengineering, including concurrent engineering—which is based on a combination of technological and managerial innovations and dematerialization of production—will transform factories, farms, and services firms.

6. Multinational firms will undergo major organizational changes. Internally, they will redesign their mass-production, single-firm organization and embark on a process of transforming themselves into networks of flexible, specialized, and interdependent autonomous production units. Externally, they will downgrade the importance of their territorial organization and management (IBM Thailand, IBM South Asia, IBM Asia, IBM World) in the decisionmaking process, and will become quasi-global networks spanning sectors and countries.

Small- and medium-size enterprises will remain the molecular texture of the economy in the technologically advanced countries as well. The separation between advanced SMEs, fully integrated in different ways into the world of the global networks of networks, and the traditional SME more locally and regionally oriented will be further accentuated.

7. If new effective measures are not applied, the main result of the processes described above will be a new wave of massive unemployment in the United States, Western Europe, and, to a lesser extent, in Japan and the four minidragons of Southeast Asia. Some recent studies anticipate that approximately 20 to 25 million jobs will be cut in the United States in the course of the next twenty years. The new wave will be exacerbated by new major flows

of immigration into the region of the triadic world. In Western Europe, for instance, immigration will come from Central and Eastern Europe, Russia, and North and Central Africa.

8. The push toward the "greening" of industry, farming, and the informal economy will represent a major source of change. Environmentally compatible processes, products, and services will be demanded and imposed. A new generation of taxes (the eco-taxes) will enrich and transform the fiscal system in technologically advanced countries. Eco-taxes will not, however, be as severe and constraining as feared by many industrialists or desired by environmentalists. Their rate of their introduction and their content will be subject to the imperative of competitiveness. The need for a country's competitiveness in order to reduce unemployment will be used as an argument against the rapid and intensive greening of industry and farming.

9. Cities and city-regions, more than national territories, will become the relevant spaces for the reindustrialization and reorganization of the globalizing economy. The leaders of cities and city-regions will increasingly play a major role in the reconstruction of urban societies.

10. Finally, national public authorities (and related intergovernmental international institutions) will tend to fluctuate between a fully fledged market-dominated economy (hence the continuing pressure in favor of privatization, deregulation, and liberalization) and tempered forms of social market economy combined with moderate protectionist policies. They will tend to consider in the next ten to fifteen years that their basic economic and industrial task is to promote and enhance the country's macro- and micro-competitiveness.

From the above, a matrix can be derived with two axes along which the future configurations of the world economy are organized. The first axis goes along the line localism/fragmentation versus the line globalization/integration that we have already described; the second axis goes along the line global governance based on market mechanisms versus global governance based on mixed, cooperative forms of economy (see figure 3.1).

**Alternative Options: Competition for Survival,**
**Pax Triadica, or Global Governance**
In the perspective of a global world dominated by the logics of fragmentation (see figure 3.2), three possible scenarios emerge. Scenario A (SA) is the extreme one. We may call it the apartheid scenario, in which the cities,

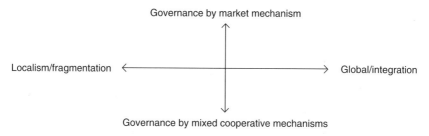

**Figure 3.1**
Toward scenarios of globalization: Alternative axes of global world configuration

regions, and countries of the most highly technoscientific developed world will evolve in such a way that they will delink from the rest of the world. The gradual delinking will be based on the increasing role of sophisticated knowledge and technology incorporated into the production processes, products, and services that will construct the new material and nonmaterial organization of the developed countries of the world, the new energy systems, the new (de)materialized economy, new information and multimedia infrastructures and services, and new advanced research organization and education systems. The developed world will follow its own development patterns and will maintain weaker and looser links with the other cities, regions, and countries, which will be faced with economic poverty, inadequate and outdated infrastructures, and the increase in local ethnic and interstate wars.

The scenario will imply the existence of a national consensus among industry, government, and labor on a kind of national pact on competitiveness for survival. The world configuration will be organized within the triadic system of competitiveness and economic wars of which a critical component will be the national systems of competitiveness. The central element of the global strategy for survival of the most advanced national systems will concern the firm's and country's positioning within the globalizing production systems. The national systems of competitiveness will be oriented to the continued rationalization of production costs. The introduction of new forms of work organization (reduction of working time, in particular) in a minority of plants and industries will confirm the leading economies' commitment to productivity-based growth and the treatment of

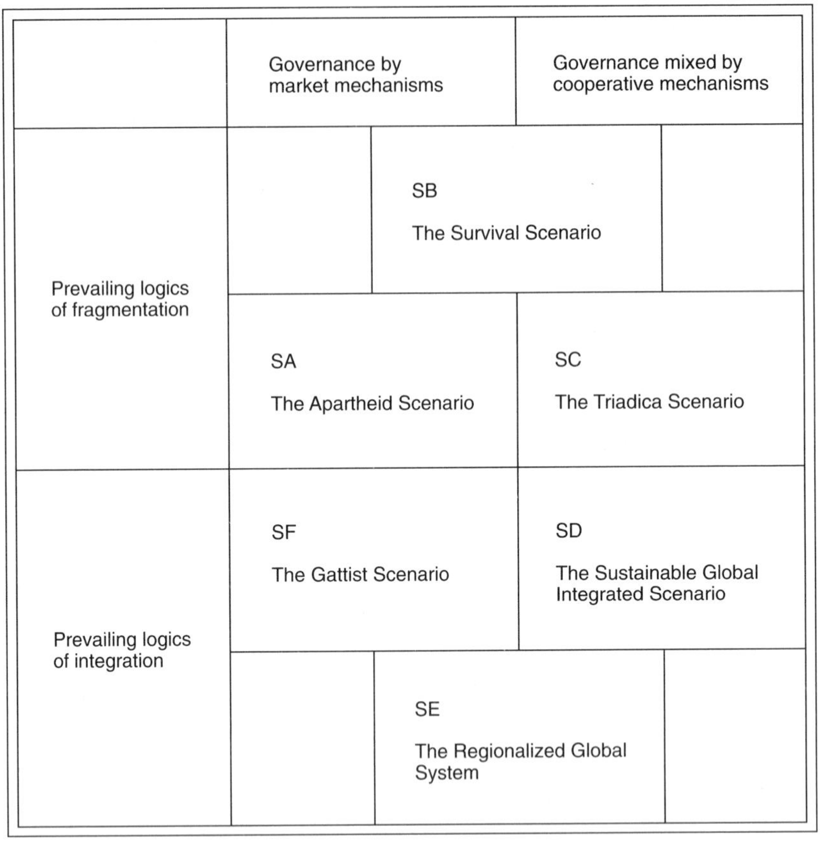

| | Governance by market mechanisms | Governance mixed by cooperative mechanisms |
|---|---|---|
| | SB<br><br>The Survival Scenario | |
| Prevailing logics of fragmentation | SA<br><br>The Apartheid Scenario | SC<br><br>The Triadica Scenario |
| | SF<br><br>The Gattist Scenario | SD<br><br>The Sustainable Global Integrated Scenario |
| Prevailing logics of integration | SE<br><br>The Regionalized Global System | |

**Figure 3.2**
Six scenarios of globalization: A static approach

highly skilled labor as a critical competitive resource. The dominant approaches to the question of labor organization, however, will remain primarily oriented to cost reduction. Offshore labor sourcing, further implementation of technology-led reorganization principally as a labor-saving device, and widespread use of contingent labor and company downsizing will constitute a far more prevalent competitiveness strategy than the reconstruction of work.

The previous chapter described an elementary form of the delinking process, highlighted by statistics from 1970 to 1990. That is, potential elements for scenario A are already at work. The apartheid scenario, however, has a very low rate of probability in general and a near-zero chance of occurrence in the next twenty years. It is rather difficult to admit that a truly extended form of world apartheid will become a reality in the short period of twenty years. Also, this kind of delinking seems impossible because even if capital does not move, people do. Migrations of people seeking jobs will be fostered. A few important elements, such as the increasing technoscientific differentiation between the developed and the nondeveloped worlds and the reduction of import/export linkages between the two, makes it plausible nevertheless.

In the long term, this scenario will be based on a kind of cultural wall that will separate the world of the integrated and the world of the excluded. The two worlds will simply coexist with minimal interaction. Migration flows will be energetically controlled. The traditional forms of representative intergovernmental organizations (one country, one vote) will become obsolete. A world directorate functioning in the manner of a board of managers will ensure that the two worlds do not enter into dangerous interactions. The world order of the fittest will prevail.

Scenario B (SB) presents a situation in which the fragmentation of the world takes place in the context of a quasi-generalized, privatized, deregulated, and liberalized market economy. We may call it the survival scenario, in which each enterprise, city, region, country, and social group looks to the defense and promotion of its own comparative advantage and acquired position.

The driving force is self-survival by means of defeating others. To win is the motivating principle, and no place is left for the losers. The imperative of competitiveness governs individual and collective behavior and strategies. Technological innovation with a view to increasing labor productivity (that is, to reduce labor costs and therefore to cut the need for employment) is considered the most effective weapon for eliminating competitors from the market.

Technology races and technology wars will introduce a high level of instability without. however, leading to full destabilization of this scenario—at least within the next twenty years. The role of buffer will be played, on the one side, by international organizations such as the IMF, World Bank, and GATT and, on the other side, by national public authorities. The latter, in fact, will consider their most useful function and industrial role in a fragmented globalized competitive economy to consist of generating the most favorable environment for the enhancement of the competitiveness of their national (local) firms. Scenario B is already largely at work. Its probability of becoming the dominant situation in the course of the next twenty years is fairly high.

Scenario C (SC) is a situation in which the fragmentation of the world takes place within a relatively stable economic order under the control of the three most developed regions (that is, North America, Western Europe, Japan, and the minidragons of Southeast Asia). We call it the pax triadica scenario.

### Pax Triadica: Toward Global Governance

The pax triadica means that the new world order that will emerge in the next twenty years will rest upon a tacit and explicit consensus between the regions of the triad on their common interest in cogoverning the world economy and society to ensure the greatest possible political stability and the highest possible rate of socioeconomic development. The pax triadica will be the result of equilibrium among the world powers. In fact, no global power—however large—will be in a position to impose its will on the others.

The United States will still hold military hegemony and remain committed to maintaining this position. The technological and economic supremacy of the United States, however, has again been seriously challenged by Japan and more recently by Western Europe. It may happen that the American economy will succeed in recapturing its preeminent position in several sectors. Even if this were to be the case, U.S. economic power at the world level would have declined in relative terms compared to today. By 2000, Japan and the four minidragons will represent 35 percent of the world's economic product, higher than the combined product of the twelve countries of the European Community and considerably higher than the total production of the United States.

Regarding Japan, it is likely that it will move further toward consolidating and expanding its position throughout the world in all key economic sectors. Japan will not lose its momentum so quickly, if ever. However, it is rather difficult to contemplate the possibility that Japan will acquire world military and political hegemony in the coming twenty to thirty years. No military revenge from Japan against China or the United States is conceivable and or would be accepted. The same applies to the possible hegemonic role of Japan within Asia. Although the other Asian countries will easily accept the leading economic strength of Japan, they will strongly resist any Japanese political or military domination of Asian economic and political organizations.

Western European countries will still be too divided on many fronts to play a hegemonic role on the world stage. The single market and the Treaty of Maastricht will have reinforced the status of the European Community as the first world trading power. It is possible that the European Community will become the first world monetary power by the end of this century, and within the following ten years the strongest political continental entity. But NATO will not disappear in the next fifteen to twenty years, and no European government or parliament will advocate that Europe should invest massively in military projects with a view to making Europe the hegemonic military power of the world by 2010–2020. Under these conditions, the United States, Western Europe, and Japan are bound to cogovern the world.

Nobody will have made the pax triadica an explicit and deliberate choice. Rather it seems to be a logical, unavoidable evolution—logical because everyone agrees that the world needs a stable order and clearly defined power relations following the collapse of the USSR, the demographic explosion (and related ethnic and religious conflicts and new massive migrations), and environmental insecurity (especially that associated with old nuclear power stations). The pax triadica will appear to be the best solution, the way to satisfy the general interest of the world population. It is assumed that the richer and more developed the members of the triad become and the more they cooperate among themselves, the more other countries will reap the benefits and the more assured world stability will be. The peaceful triadic world trade system will enrich everyone.

The pax triadica will be blessed by scientific and technological modernity. Contrary to the previous world order based on the balance of terror, the pax triadica will be based on a reduction of the armaments race and on greater mobilization of scientific and technological potential for civilian purposes, although it will still allow for huge military expenditures and a rejuvenated high-tech, less labor-intensive military industry and army. Equally, it will operate with the maintenance and expansion of intensive economic competitiveness for the acquisition of the strongest market position at the world level. The trade wars that will continue to mark the relations between the United States and Japan, or Japan and Western Europe, and the United States and Western Europe will coexist with the superior common interest and the level of interdependence that strongly links the three superpowers. In this sense, the pax triadica will tend to strengthen the integration processes among the members of the triad. As was the case with pax romana, the pax triadica will imply a division between citizens (that is, those who are recognized as having the privilege to be members of the integrated world) and the barbarians (the excluded).

Many important elements of the pax triadica scenario are already at work: the G7 for instance is one instrument of the desired world economic order. The same applies to the increasing use in some sectors of cooperative links between multinational corporations at the world level—as illustrated by the strategic alliance signed by IBM/Toshiba and Siemens—and in other sectors of a more protectionist type of behavior.

In a world in which the processes, mechanisms, and institutions of integration will increase, three other scenarios are highly conceivable.

Scenario D (SD), like scenario A, is an extreme one. We call it the sustainable global integration scenario in which the principle of global common good, human solidarity, wealth sharing, global social and environmental accountability, dialogue of cultures, respect for human rights, and universal tolerance are gradually translated into daily life at the company, city, national, continental, and institutional levels.

SD is based on the recognition that global problems are so vast that the only way to cope with them is to design new rules and strategies and to develop at the appropriate levels those mechanisms, procedures, and institutions that will enable effective global governance. The imperative of free-market competitiveness is replaced by the imperative of a socially and environmentally accountable cooperative economy. The synthesis of know-how, expertise, and local solutions from countries and regions all over the world through pluralist forms of technological, economic, and social development projects is one of the basic mechanisms in support of SD.

The probability of this scenario occuring in the course of the next twenty years is extremely low. There are, however, several signs that indicate the emergence of some processes and mechanisms that are conditionally necessary to the realization of SD. There is the case, for instance, of the organization in Rio de Janeiro in June 1992 of the United Nations Conference on Environment and Development that represented—as noted earlier—the first attempt at global negotiation on the conditions and means for the production and distribution of wealth at the world level. The conference in Rio also produced Agenda 21, which, despite its many limitations and structural weaknesses, represents a "plan for the development of the world economy in the mutual interest of all countries" and, if applied, could give birth to a new generation of institutions for global governance.

Scenario E (SE) characterizes a situation in which the process and institutionalization of an integrated world economy takes the form of a unique integrated market, that is, a replication at the world level of the single European market that was established by the European Community on January 1, 1993. It may be called the Gattist scenario, in other words, a scenario based on a world economy functioning according to the full realization of the principles of the GATT.

Like the single European market, this single global market will imply free circulation of goods, services, capital, and people. Of course, such a single global market will demand a new global context among all the signatories of the present GATT. It will presuppose radical changes in many policy areas such as banking, insurance, monetary and fiscal regulation, agriculture, and social security. A considerable number of multicountry and multisector trade agreements will have to disappear, and strong antitrust regulations and institutions will have to be created.

Taken together, this makes this apparently plausible scenario rather unrealistic within the period of fifteen to twenty years. Nevertheless, this scenario is based on actual processes, and coherently reflects the philosophy behind the GATT as well as the current trends in favor of global deregulation and liberalization. The difficulty of carrying out the Uruguay Round within the GATT rules highlights the tension between those who (sometimes self-interestedly) defend the extreme application of those rules to agriculture and services, and those who consider the Gattist scenario unacceptable (perhaps for equally self-serving reasons).

Scenario F (SF) is one where the processes and institutionalization of an integrated world economy are based on a two-tiered cooperative integration. The first is at the continental level. Hence SF will be based on regional integrated units such as the European Community, the Great Maghreb, the North American Free Trade Area (NAFTA), Mercosur (Latin America), the new Community of Independent States (the former Soviet Union), the Asian

Free Trade Area (AFTA), and so on. These regional units carry different degrees of economic and political integration. The second is at the level of the planet, based on cooperation among the various regionally integrated units. To this end, an important reorganization of present international institutions such as the IMF, World Bank, and GATT will have to occur. The same applies to the United Nations organization and the various organizations of the United Nations family such as UNESCO, FAO, ILO, and the WHO.

The world is moving in this direction as far as the process of regional integration is concerned, although one cannot guarantee that the model of regional integration will spread everywhere—including Africa, Central Asia, the Indian subcontinent, and Latin America—to a significantly high degree. What is evident is that regional economic integration is most advanced in Western Europe, North America, and East and Southeast Asia.

This static description of the scenarios does not tell us enough about the possible evolution of the global economy and society and the mix of inter-actions and cross-impacts that will occur between the different logics, forces, and players associated with the six scenarios. Figure 3.3 is an attempt to provide a dynamic view of the scenarios. The current processes of reorga-nization suggest that one of two scenarios are the most probable in the course of the next fifteen to twenty years: the survival scenario (SB) and the regional integration scenario (SF). The latter is, in our view, more desirable than the former. If the survival scenario prevails, which is highly likely if present trends and policies continue, the question is whether it will evolve sooner or later into scenario A (global apartheid) or scenario C (pax triadica) or, preferably, into scenario E or scenario D—the most desirable scenario but, conversely, the least probable within the next twenty-five to thirty years. A careful analysis of each basic assumption against current trends suggests that the pax triadica scenario could become the most probable in ten to fifteen years' time, a natural evolution from the survival scenario.

To sum up, the options for the next fifteen to twenty years seem to lie along three different routes: the survival scenario, the pax triadica scenario, and the regionalized global system scenario as a positive move toward a cooperative global integration scenario. For the time being, the predominant choice in the search for new rules for the governance of the global world emphasizes competitiveness, that is, the survival scenario.

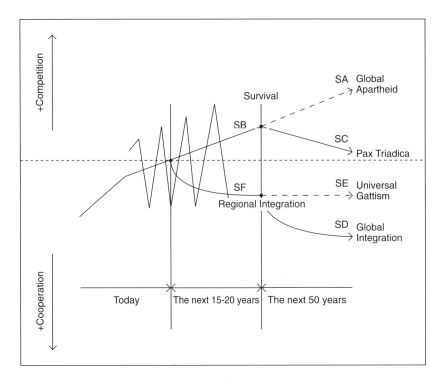

**Figure 3.3**
Six scenarios of globalization: A dynamic approach

## The Predominant Answer: Competitiveness

Competitiveness is currently the predominant credo. Maintaining and increasing the competitiveness of firms and the national economy is considered the best way to assure the most efficient governance of the world economy and the highest level of social well-being. It is certainly the case that economic competitiveness has much to recommend it.

### The Value of Competition

Competition is an essential dimension of social organized life. It is also a natural phenomenon in economic life as well as a major source of wealth generation. Competing for the exploitation of natural resources and the generation of new artificial resources to satisfy individual and collective needs at lower costs and higher quality has contributed significantly to the increase of the material and nonmaterial level of wealth and the promotion of a better quality of life. Competition, as one of the driving forces behind technological innovation and productivity growth, has lifted human aspirations and made possible high records of achievements.[1]

Classical economic theory suggests that in a situation where all economic agents have equal access to limited natural resources, competition will ensure their optimal exploitation to the benefit of all agents. The reality, however, has never conformed to this theory. Nevertheless, competition has played a fundamental role in the growth of our economies and in socioeconomic progress.

Above all, the introduction of free and open competition in political life has been the basis for the development and expansion of democratic systems—one of the greatest social achievements in the history of humankind. Autocracy may give the impression of being the most efficient system of power for a while. But in the long term, no country has been able to survive as a progressive and economically innovative system in the absence of free competition for power. The inner strength of competition, which explains its great value for society, lies in the fact that competition essentially means "to seek together" (from Latin: *cum petere*)—to seek together the best solution to the right problem, in the right place and at the right time. It also means that the selection of the best is not reduced to the unique. In any international competition—be it a movie festival or a musical event—there are prizes for several winners.

This is one element of the competition story; another is that competition has also been increasingly associated in the past, under the influence of economic thinking and practice, with the notion of a contest between rivals. A typical recent illustration of this link is the advertising campaign of the Peugeot 306, based on the concept that this car is "La Rivale" (the rival).

## Competition Transformed: The Competition Ideology— From Means to Ends

A new competition era, however, has emerged in the last twenty to thirty years, and globalization has been a contributing factor. As we have seen, globalization has changed the setting of economic activities. As a result of the move from territorially defined national economies to the open space of

global economies, globalization is raising the possibility that global competition could lead to global dominance. It also raises the stakes—as the
economies and societies of the world became both more interdependent and
concerned by uneven relationships of power, a major spillover effect in
competition is taking place; that is, you cannot compete in one area without
competing in all areas, an effect that in its turn amplifies the possibility of
global dominance.[2]

Competitiveness has become the primary goal of industrialists, bankers,
and governmental trade and industry departments. Industrialists, politicians,
economists, financial leaders, technologists, and trade unionists have
adopted the competitiveness metaphor as their credo. The imperative of
competitiveness is the center of their discussions and propositions. No other
word is used as frequently in political speeches, newspapers, books, and
business management courses and seminars. The battle for competitiveness
is the most discussed international economic conern of the last twenty years.

How to address people's concerns about employment? The answer is:
"Increase competitiveness." (This explains the title of a 1994 British government paper, "Competitiveness and Employment.") How should university curricula be modified and why? The answer is: "Adjust the curricula to
the needs of industry in order to make it more competitive." How to
foster better development and use of technology? The answer is: "Focus
on competitiveness."

Did the European Community approve a common Research and Technology Policy for the first time in its history in 1985? The sole objective of the
new policy was "to improve the scientific basis of European industry with a
view to strengthening its competitiveness at the international level."

"Competing with Technology" is the title of a report of the Dutch government to the parliament that was made public in June 1993, in which an
outlook for the technology policy in the Netherlands is given. The main
purpose is to improve the Netherlands' position in the technology race.

The same cultural background is behind "Train to Compete," the slogan
used by Berlitz-Belgium to promote its six-month intensive Japanese language program, *"Apprender à Competir "*(Learn to Be Competitive), the
motto used by the "Euroforum University" created by the Complutenses
University in El Escorial, and the position supported by the Industrial R&D
Advisory Committee of the Commission of the European Union.

The supporters of the competitiveness credo are deeply convinced that the competitive market economy is the only efficient answer to the problems and challenges facing the economies and societies of the world. Their conviction applies not only to the most developed countries but to all countries, regions, and firms of the world. Accordingly, in their opinion, the increased participation in the free market by African countries and firms is considered the answer to the problems of growing impoverishment and sociopolitical dislocation of the African continent. The same solution is suggested for Latin America. Equally, they believe the fight against the ecological disruption of the planet can be won via greater freedom for competitive firms: if market forces are fully liberated to do their job, the mechanisms of competitiveness will ensure the necessary equilibria between costs and prices. Environmental costs, for example, will be internalized by firms; this will lead to real pricing, and gradually environmentally friendly processes and products will be preferred by consumers and investors.

The complete liberalization of world trade in all sectors, based on GATT principles, is seen as the necessary condition, provided that everybody applies the principles in an integral and fair manner. The universal extension and application of the principles and rules of a competitive market economy to govern the world economy and society is considered the most effective solution, because defining and applying democratic governance of the world based on global rules and procedures seems extremely difficult and unrealistic. Therefore, in the absence of such rules and procedures, the only democratic way—we are told—is to let market forces decide, that is, to leave it to the most competitive firms, regions, and countries to tell the world where to go and the best way to get there. Within such a context, the strategic role given to the state and the international intergovernmental organizations requires the following:

● the state must create the most favorable economic and sociopolitical environment at the national level to promote and enhance the international competitiveness of firms and the entire national economy;

● the international intergovernmental organizations such as the GATT, IMF, World Bank, FAO, UNESCO, and UNIDO have to support and strengthen all forms of cooperation that are favorable to the expansion of the principles and rules of the free competitive market economy, and at the same time are intended to promote more balanced North-South relations and better environmentally and socially sustainable development.

Among the questions we are seeking answers to are: Why has competitiveness become such a predominant credo? Why is the objective of commercial competitiveness more important in the minds of private and public decisionmakers than any other objective? How is it possible that a means, a modality (competition between firms and economic agents), has become the primary goal for all economic agents and the entire society?

That fair competition among firms is one of the guiding principles governing the functioning of the economy is understandable; similarly, competition is a natural constraint for those economic agents operating in market sectors. Within clearly defined rules of economic functioning and behavior, competition is a necessary and unavoidable condition for ensuring that goods and services are designed, developed, and produced with the highest return to investors and to the greatest satisfaction of consumers, while contributing to the improvement of the general economic and social well-being of the population and to the environmentally sound development of the economy. Competition is a powerful instrument for innovation. It stimulates the search for cheaper and better processes, products, and services. It tends to ensure the closest and most effective links between the producer and the consumer. In principle, competition makes the pull of demand the driving force of economic innovation.

As with any one-sided vision and ideology, the dogma of competitiveness is based on a few simplistic notions.[4] The main foundation is the conception that our economies and our societies are engaged in a technological, industrial, and economic war at the global level; hence the main objective is to become strong enough to defeat the competitors. For the Americans, the main competitors are the Japanese and Western Europeans. For the Japanese, they are the Western Europeans and the Americans. For the Western Europeans, they are the other Western Europeans, the Japanese, and the Americans.[5] For the South Koreans, the main competitors are Japan, Singapore, Taiwan, and increasingly mainland China. The conviction that our societies are fully involved in a merciless economic war has gained momentum, seemingly coinciding with the end of the cold war. Knowing whether this is due to a casual coincidence or to a more profound collective sociopsychology (that is, organized populations need external enemies) is important, but the facts remain.

Business leaders are among the strongest supporters of the idea that today's world is characterized and dominated by an economic war. "We have to face an economic war," insists Louis Gallois, CEO of Aerospatiale, the well-known French manufacturer of Airbus, missiles, and helicopters. In Gallois's view, the warlike development of global economies is modifying the type of interfirm alliances that are formed. In the past, he says, alliances were made on programs and new product developments and each partner retained its independence. "Today the priority goal of alliances is to reduce costs and to improve our competitiveness."[6] Politicians are equally convinced. France's former President Mitterand, the United States' President Clinton, and Germany's Chancellor Kohl often make reference to the existence of an economic war. Although they deplore it, they accept it as a fact that people have to live with—but in such a way that their citizens are among the winners. That there are "winners" is another way of suggesting that our societies are involved in a merciless economic war. "Winning in a World Economy" was the title of a report adopted by the Science Council of Canada, which was devoted to the role of university-industry interaction for the economic renewal in Canada.[7] Winning is a fundamental component of American culture. It has become the flagship of American business. According to the General Electric management approach, a decision in favor of the development of a new product has to respond to five questions, especially the last two:

- what do we want to be? (vision)
- what are we going to do? (mission)
- what do we believe? (values)
- where are we going to win? (objectives)
- how are we going to win? (strategies)[8]

It is known that the principle applied by General Electric is to remain active in a sector if the company is number one or two. If not, it sells off its interest in that sector.

The greater the competitiveness of a firm, region, or country, the greater will be its chance of survival. The lack of competitiveness means exclusion from the market, the loss of mastery over the future, and submission to the domination of the stronger. Individual and collective socioeconomic well-being, the autonomy of a region, the security and independence of a country or a continent are all dependent on the degree of competitiveness.

The credo of competitiveness has its evangelists, theologians, priests, and, evidently, its followers. The followers are the millions of people in the developed regions and groups of the world, especially within the triad. The evangelists are those thousands of economists and experts from the United States, Western Europe, and more recently from Japan, Taiwan, Singapore, and South Korea who have codified and established—by virtue of their scientific authority—the natural-law character of the principles and mechanisms of the modern capitalist market economy. In doing so, they have introduced into the popular conception of the contemporary economy a series of ideas and themes borrowed, rightly or wrongly, from other scientific and philosophic realms: from Hobbes comes "Homo homini lupus"; from Darwin, evolution based on natural selection; and from Nietzsche, the dramatic character of the human condition and the sense of being a winner.

The ranks of theologians mushroomed during the 1970s and 1980s, producing a vast body of literature. A library data search on the words "competitiveness" and "competition" (limited to their use in the last fifteen years in English writing) would produce several thousand pages of references. In their textbooks, the theologians have explained that competitiveness is not only an objective for a firm (microcompetitiveness), an industrial sector (mesocompetitiveness), or a country (macrocompetitiveness), but that it concerns everyone, including the state, the education system, the health system, and the trade unions.[9]

The priests of the cult of competitiveness are found everywhere—on university campuses, parliaments, in cities from London to São Paulo, at the International Monetary Fund and the Commission of the European Community, in the chambers of commerce of Oslo, Cairo, and Calcutta as well as in the German trade unions. They are now even spreading throughout China. Among the priests, the business and management consultants are the most convinced group and the best equipped to convince others. The teaching and promotion of the credo provides them with a most comfortable source of income. The cult has its own "scientific" instrument: the World

Competitiveness Index (WCI).[10] This index has been compiled for several years by a private Swiss institution, the World Economic Forum, with the assistance of the Institute for Management Development in Lausanne. Every year, the WCI ranks all countries of the world according to their degree of competitiveness (one major indicator is the degree of commercial and industrial aggressiveness). Naturally, Japan has been at the top of the WCI ranking system during recent years.

To assess a country's competitiveness and suggest ways to enhance it has become a nationally institutionalized task in many countries. In Belgium, for instance, the Central Economy Council, an influential multipartite organization, has to produce a report every six months on the competitiveness of Belgian firms. The report is the result of joint evaluation and debate between government, industry, and trade unions. Today Belgian firms' competitiveness is the only goal that achieves full consensus among industries, trade unions, governments, and consumers. Interdepartmental groups on competitiveness have been set up in the United Kingdom, Japan, the Netherlands, and Spain. In the United States, a Competitiveness Policy Council was in operation during the Bush administration, under the chairmanship of Vice President Quayle. President Clinton has maintained the council, whose function is to produce a report every two years that is submitted to the president and the Congress. The 1993 report is called *A Competitive Strategy for America*.[11] In addition, President Clinton has created an Economic Security Council whose main task is precisely to ensure the promotion of the competitiveness of the American economy. A new report has been published by the Ente Nationale per le Energie Alternative (ENEA), Italy's largest public research organization, called *Primo Rapporto dell'ENEA sulla Competitività dell'Italia nelle Industrie ad Alta Tecnologia* (First Report from ENEA on Italy's Competitivity in High-Tech Industries). At the request of a group of European executives, a survey report was published by Booz-Allen & Hamilton and the European Business Press Federation in 1992 entitled *The Competitiveness of Europe and Its Enterprises*. The main proposal of the chief executives of the seventeen largest European corporations, in a document presented to the president of the European Commission in November 1993, was the creation of a European Council of Competitiveness comprising industrialists, politicians, and scientists (labor unionists were excluded).[12]

### The Limits of Competition Ideology: Excess Competition

Despite its popularity, competitiveness is far from being an effective answer to the present problems and opportunities of the new global world and society. Excess competition is even a source of adverse effects. The most striking result of the competition ideology is that it generates a structural distortion in the functioning of the economy itself, not to mention its devastating social effects.

First, it has become increasingly evident to many Americans that "the international economic competition of the past decade has proved a competition in terminating jobs and reducing living standards. Europeans are only now beginning to realize that the search for international competitiveness is being conducted at an unacceptable human cost."[13] Productive economic competition comes from technological improvement and rationalized industry. Increasing the number of jobless is not the way for a country to grow richer. Nor is impoverishing those with jobs by cutting wages and benefits a socially acceptable form of productivity increase.

The first result of the competitive war ideology is that the "North Americans, Europeans and Japanese are all competing by sacrificing the interests of the most vulnerable people in their societies."[14] Recently, a supporter of the ideology of competitiveness expressed the same idea in a different way. He questioned how British firms could be competitive vis-à-vis South Korea, Indonesia, or China if social protection in Europe were not further reduced and wages remained thirty, forty, or fifty times higher than those in the Asian countries. As we have seen in the previous chapter, the answer given by economic and political leaders has been to favor the reduction of social protection and real wages. How is it possible, however, to believe that there is a reasonable solution to competition between one country in which the average person works 2,200 hours per year for $1,000 and another in which individuals work 1,600 hours for $30,000? Under these conditions, it is simply demagoguery to claim that the competitiveness of the latter will be increased by a reduction in labor costs.

The second result is that if everyone is competing against everyone else, the value of competitiveness is ultimately lost. As Emile Van Lennep, the former secretary general of the OECD, correctly pointed out a decade ago in rejecting competitiveness as the only solution, "against whom should the

OECD as a whole be more competitive? Against the developing world? Against the moon?"[15] "We cannot," Samuel Brittan argues today, "all be competitive against each other."[16] If everyone competes against each other, sooner or later the system will collapse. To survive, the system needs a diverse multiplicity of players. The logic of competitiveness leads to reducing diversity within the system by eliminating all those who are unable to resist the dominant forces. In this sense, it contributes to the development of social exclusion: the noncompetitive people, firms, cities, and nations are left behind. They are no longer the subject of history.

The third effect of the ideology of competitiveness is that it is blinkered. It sees only one dimension of human and social history, that is, the spirit of competition. The spirit of competition and aggression is a powerful engine for action, motivation, and innovation. It does not, however, act in isolation nor is it disconnected from other engines such as the spirit of cooperation and solidarity. Cooperation is also a fundamental phenomenon in human history, produced and determined by society. Competition and cooperation as well as aggressiveness and solidarity are two coexisting, very often conflicting, dimensions of the human condition. The ideology of competitiveness either ignores or devalues cooperation, or it instrumentalizes it to its own logic, as is the case in the great majority of interfirm strategic alliances.

The fourth result is reductionism and sectarian fundamentalism. The ideology of competitiveness not only has just one eye, but it is a bad eye. It does not view at the right scale even the limited things it does see. Competitiveness reduces the entire process of the human condition to the perceptions, motivations, and behavior of *Homo economicus* as *Homo competitor*. All the perceptions, motivations, and behaviors either have no value—unless they are subordinated and legitimized by competitiveness—or they are irrelevant for the economy. The typical magic formula of the ideology of economically dominated competitiveness is "Let's get back to business." This formula assumes that when people get back to business, they only talk or do the correct, relevant things.

The ideology of competitiveness does not acknowledge that the market is not the only thing that determines economic development and social well-being. Though the free market has prevailed in the late 1980s, there is no certainty that the market system can cope with the extraordinary tensions that result from the acceleration of, for instance, population growth and environmental degradation. Most marketing feelers are focused on the wealthiest top billion. The market is mostly blind to the aspirations of several billion less wealthy people.

The issue is not to oppose market and nonmarket forces and argue about what is more important. The argument is that both are critical and that it is the balanced relations between them that are of paramount importance. The more the ideology of competitiveness fails to see everything and sees inadequately what it does, the more it claims that what it sees is the exclusive ultimate reality. Competitiveness fundamentalists are aggressive in their theory, blind in their approach, and sectarian in their judgment. Ultimately they can become arrogant.

In fact, there are structural limits to overruling competition, inasmuch as it does not address major challenges of:

- economic distortion;
- socioeconomic inequalities within and between nations, and the marginalization of large parts of the world;
- the exploitation of, and damage to, global life support systems (for example, growing desertification, soil erosion, extinction of animal and vegetable species, sea and river pollution);
- the concentration of power in largely unaccountable economic units (multiterritorial multinational firms, global information and communication networks).

Competition among firms alone cannot deal efficiently with the long-term issues of the world problematic. The market cannot properly take account of the future: it is by nature shortsighted. Putting together thousands of myopic organizations does not make them—individually or collectively—able to see the reality and acquire a sense of direction, nor to provide governance, order, and security with any degree of long-term awareness. The same applies to competition between nation-states. Overemphasis on competition inevitably leads to global economic wars. It exacerbates the inability of national authorities to address the right priorities at the right national and global level.

All in all, where the interests of competing firms are associated with the interests of competing nations, the result is a counterintuitive evolution against market mechanisms, for example:

- new forms of protectionism or of defensive industrial policies. To ease the ability to compete with other nations, the state aids its local firms by offering protection or artificial advantages;
- technonationalism, by restricting the movement of knowledge as possible competitive production factors in other nations;
- bilateralism, as a way to collude to keep competitors out of the market.

In other words, market competition alone is self-defeating in the context of competing nations. The same applies to market competition in a world of competing regional blocs. It seems that an efficient system of competitive markets requires a cooperative framework among nations at the global level, that is, socially accountable and politically democratic forms of global governance.

In an internationally controversial essay, "Competitiveness: A Dangerous Obsession," Paul Krugman clearly shows that "competitiveness is a meaningless word when applied to national economies."[17] More broadly, he makes three points: "[He] argues that concerns about competitiveness are, as an empirical matter, almost completely unfounded. Second, [he] tries to explain why defining the economic problems as one of international competition in nonetheless so attractive to so many people. Finally, [he] argues that the obsession with competitiveness is not only wrong but dangerous, skewing domestic policies and threatening the international economic system. Thinking in terms of competitiveness leads, directly and indirectly, to bad economic policies on a wide range of issues, domestic and foreign, whether it be in health care or trade."[18] Furthermore, the ideology of competitiveness gives priority to tools and technical systems. When thinking about what the factory of the year 2005 might be like, the first image that comes to mind is that of a more sophisticated system of machines (robots, numerical machine-control tools, flexible cells, computer-integrated manufacturing) and fewer people. Attention to people is given mostly when considering how to adjust their skills to the requirements of new technology. When thinking about the telecommunications and mass media of the future, the focus is on communication centers, switching equipment, "intelligent" terminals, networks, computers, fiber optics, the superhighway of broadband communications, satellites, cables. Only later comes concern about the role of people, and even then it is in a restricted way, that is, as producers and consumers. In this way, the ideology of competitiveness consecrates the primacy of the short term and of financial costs and benefits. The logic of monthly reports predominates. The myopic intent of shareholders prevails. The predominance of short-term objectives induces overproduction in one region and shortages in another. Even R&D activities are permeated by a financial logic that takes the lead over the industrial and political logic. Because of this "rationalization," the blind competitiveness imperative following mergers and acquisitions leads to the abandonment of R&D facilities that in many cases are still profitable.

By giving exclusive priority to excellence, competitiveness maintains and strengthens structural inequality among regions and within and across countries. There is a high degree of consensus among analysts that the single market established in January 1993 and the monetary and economic union to follow by 1997 will reinforce the existing inequalities among the regions of the European Community if the logic of competitiveness and the internal European free market is left alone, in the absence, among other things, of a common European fiscal policy.[19] The same applies to the inequalities among countries at the global level. Hypercompetitiveness has made the economically strong and rich country stronger and richer by favoring economic integration at the world level among the most developed countries. The few exceptions that are regularly mentioned in argument—that is, the four minidragons of Southeast Asia—are precisely an exception to the rule because they are not examples of the application of competitiveness. Their fast growth and commercial success are mainly due to the fact that they have been in the course of the last forty years—for economic and political/strategic reasons—the new sites of investment and localization of growth of multinational firms from the most developed countries. Western firms, from a social and political perspective, have found in these countries an extremely favorable climate (that is, cheap labor, weakness or absence of trade unions, stable authoritarian political regimes).

The inequalities in the economy are also cross-impacted and amplified by the social inequalities and exclusions created by the ideology of competition. Armed with only the truth of market laws, competitiveness creates fundamental exclusion among economic agents: everybody is invited to lunch, but only a few individuals, firms, social groups, and regions will have legitimate access to the table, that is, those who have been able to acquire their access ticket by being more competitive than the others. Only the winners have the right to continue to fight for future conquests. Increasingly, the logic of the winner is accepted and internalized. And increasingly less genuine, dense, visible, and durable are the social links and the sense of belonging among individuals, villages, social groups, cities, and countries. The common good and the general interest are reduced to those of the winning multinational firms engaged in technological and economic wars in the global economy. Once more, women and ethnic minorities are the most affected and sacrificed social groups. The ideology of competitiveness exacerbates problems of identity of all kinds, because it tends to pit people against each other.

Under these conditions, it is very difficult to talk about the existence of democratic institutions and regimes. Formal democracy may exist, but no substantive democracy where the logic of economic wars and the law of the strongest predominate and the rights of the weaker are limited to those of being a good production soldier (if the chance of having access to a job is given) and a consumer (within the limits of reasonable costs for public poverty assistance) (see box 3.2).

Finally, the ideology of competitiveness leads to large-scale cultural impoverishment, as illustrated by present widespread analyses and debates on issues related to science, technology, wealth, ethics, democracy, the environment, North–South relations, and peace and solidarity. Everything is reduced to a few simple slogans centered on the firms, market, management, efficiency, productivity, innovation, transfer of technology, commercialization, power, and customers.

Today's societies are confronted, mutatis mutandis, with the same problem that last century's societies were confronted with and have, to some degree, been successful in solving, especially from the post–World War II period. The problem then was the excesses of capitalism. Nineteenth-century attempts to promote representative democracy and improve the social conditions of workers and employees, as well as twentieth-century efforts, have been directed toward counterbalancing these excesses. Thus,

- against the tendency of capitalism to reduce competition (monopoly capitalism), antitrust laws were enacted;
- against the tendency to exploit labor, laws were enforced preventing child labor, regulating working conditions, providing for minimum wages;

**Box 3.2**
The negative effects of excess competition

---

- Gives priority to tools and technical systems rather than to people and human organizations. People are relevant only as producers and consumers.
- Gives primacy to short-term financial costs. Creates overproduction and shortages.
- Reduces the competitive character of the domestic national market and increases industrial and financial concentrations at the global level. In doing so, favors the development of global oligopolistic markets.
- Strengthens regional inequality within and across countries in access to the innovation process (the rich and strong become richer and stronger).
- Strengthens the division of the world population and regions into the "integrated" world and the "excluded" world.
- Contributes to a high level of environmental disruption, though it can stimulate the search for new processes and products.
- Is a source of major social exclusion. The noncompetitive people, firms, cities, and nations are left behind. They are no longer the subject of history. They are worthless because they are the "losers."
- Supports the cycle of individual and collective aggressiveness and prevents the development of solidarity and dialogue between people, nations, and communities.
- Reduces the capability of public organizations and representative democracy at local, national, and global levels.

---

- against the tendency to exclude, social welfare programs were set up;
- against the tendency to deceive, truth-in-advertising laws and consumer protection regulations were established;
- and, more recently, against the tendency to externalize environmental costs, environmental protection regulations have been enacted.

These achievements contributed to the gradual establishment of the national social contract that formed the basis of the modern economic and social development of advanced Western societies. The state, as promoter and guarantor of the public general interest, intervened. The excesses of national competitive capitalism were softened. This took place within a national framework, where the nation-state had the ability to influence the operations and evolution of national capitalism.

Today the source of the problem is the same, that is, globalizing competitive capitalism has its excesses, but the framework of its operations and the role of the key players, in particular the nation-state, has changed. Because of the erosion of national markets, inter alia, the state has become a weakened instrument against the forces of globalization, whereas the networks of multinational corporations have seen their ability to influence and control increase significantly. This creates a serious problem because many of the excesses of competitive capitalism are reemerging on a global scale. For instance:

- in the context of market deregulation and liberalization, financial and industrial capital mobility at the world level is bypassing the regulatory framework based on the nation-state;
- in a growing number of financial and industrial sectors there is a strong tendency toward oligopolistic structures. Regional and global interfirm alliances and mergers are permitted on the basis of the argument that one has to favor a nation's or region's competitiveness at the global level;
- labor legislation and social welfare programs are weakened or slowly dismantled; mass unemployment will become one of the major social issues of the next fifteen to twenty years, and enhancing local firms' competitiveness is claimed to be the best way to re-create jobs within a particular country;
- indifference to those excluded is again on the rise (growing social exclusion, intolerance, delinking between regions);
- moratoria or cancellation of regulations concerning environmental protection are increasingly demanded, for the sake of competitiveness.

**Competition Cannot Govern the Planet**
On the basis of the preceding it is possible to answer the question, "Can competition govern the planet?" The answer is that it cannot. Competition is clearly an inadequate response to the new forms of coexistence and codevelopment required by a finite world and an increasingly interdependent and interactive global system. The role of competitiveness as a modality of a specific market configuration has to be rethought and redefined in light of the conditions and dynamics of the new global world.

Competitiveness has a limited contribution to make in terms of efficiency vis-à-vis the provision of socially pertinent and environmentally friendly goods and services to satisfy the basic needs and aspirations of a "have not" population of between 3 and 5 billion people in the course of a generation or two. Competitiveness is proving to be neither an efficient nor effective instrument for the solution of urban maldevelopment, unemployment, and uneven wealth distribution in the advanced developed countries of the triad. One of the greatest weaknesses of competitiveness is that it is unable to reconcile social justice, economic efficiency, environmental sustainability, political democracy, and cultural diversity in today's world. Clearly, we have to find a more effective and reliable alternative.

# 4

## Toward Effective Global Governance

### Cooperative Governance

#### Process and Approaches

By comparing the most probable scenarios of the new global world in the making, the survival scenario, based on the predominance of the principle of competitiveness, is not the most effective way to meet the needs and aspirations of the majority of the world's population. Competitiveness cannot be the guiding principle governing the visions, strategies, and actions of people in this transition period. It is powerless vis-à-vis the major socioeconomic global problems confronting us today, including growing poverty, delinking between the rich countries and the rest of the world, and environmental degradation. Two scenarios emerge as the most desirable: the regionalized global scenario and the sustainable global integrated scenario. Both resort to the predominance of the logic of integration (rather than fragmentation) and of the principle of global governance by mixed cooperative mechanisms (rather than governance by market mechanisms only). Within the context of the two scenarios, the new global world will be the result of cooperative construction processes based on the enhancement of the principles, rules, and institutions—such as freedom, democracy, solidarity, social justice, economic efficiency—that have marked the history of the twentieth century and that have attempted to counteract the influence of other principles, rules, and institutions such as autocracy, oligarchy, social Darwinism, economic alienation, cultural intolerance, and aggressive nationalism.

Contrary to the survival scenario, which implies that only the winners will construct the new global world, cooperation will offer humankind improved opportunities to cope with the forces of fragmentation and delinking represented by the demographic explosion of the poor, drugs, nuclear proliferation, speculative monetary movements, ethnic and religious fundamentalism, AIDS, global warming, and massive population migrations. To cope with such forces and promote a better governance of the world, there exists a considerable number of reasonable and constructive proposals, programs, and projects. The issue is not the absence of ideas on what should be done. Nor is there a shortage of specific, concrete programs for action. One may reasonably say that despite all that is known, there is always room for identifying new ideas. The issue at stake is the how: how to find the way(s) to define and agree on the central modalities and means that should guide the process toward an effective global governance and, more important, how to make the new values, instruments, and institutions work. Toward this end, two fundamental questions have to be answered: Which is (are) the most crucial process(es) that should be promoted? And what are the most promising approaches to follow with a view to finding the way(s)?

The key process seems to be establishing a contract, that is, the process of reaching a decision among concerned parties along the lines of the global common good, including commonly defined objectives for coexistence and mutual development. The creation of the United Nations fifty years ago is an example of a contract signed at the world level by the most influential powers. They reached agreement on the main purpose of the reconstruction of a postwar world and, more specifically, on the rules and mechanisms to be adopted to achieve that aim and to further consolidate the new postwar world. A new contract is needed for our time that would define the main aim, rules, and mechanisms for the reconstruction of the post–cold war world as well as that of a world beyond the present competitive economic war.

Two main approaches are currently proposed. The first approach is regionalization, that is, building on existing regional, economic, and political entities in various parts of the world. The regional units are regarded as the pillars of a new global system based on (relatively) balanced relationships among comparable regional units, sharing interregional governing rules and institutions at the global level. The global system that would eventually emerge from regionalization would not be a United Nations system composed of a large number of nation-states considered to be sovereign and to have equal voice in the system. The new system would resemble a United

Federations, composed of a few regional units (unions, confederations, federations). The second approach is globalization, that is, the establishment of rules, mechanisms, and government-type institutions at the global level that would enable local, national, and regional entities and processes to interact and converge toward an effective governance of the global society. In the minds of many supporters of the globalization approach, the system that could emerge would be neither an enhancement of the present United Nations system nor the expansion and consolidation at a political level of an integrated global market. The globalization approach implies the adoption of significantly new rules, mechanisms, and institutions that would meet the requirements and conditions associated with the global dimension taken by the course of human affairs, problems, opportunities, and prospects.

Although regionalization and globalization have much in common (some regard regionalization as just a step on the path toward globalization), the two approaches are in fact quite distinct. They imply different types of organization of the global system, as well as different sets of identified interests, rules, mechanisms, individual and collective visions, strategies, and behaviors.

## The Contract: More Than a Necessity—A Choice

The search for a new contract at the global level is very often presented as necessary if our societies wish to avoid major global disasters. Sometimes the global contract is justified as the last opportunity offered to humankind for assuring its own survival.[1] There is much truth in this view. Undoubtedly, the urgent need for global action to prevent major ecological, social, economic, and political disasters is a fact. History suggests that the perception of major threats to survival is not sufficient to produce constructive action; civilizations, empires, and institutions have collapsed despite the awareness of major threats. And often the same people who are in fact able to mobilize themselves against threats to their survival are ill-prepared to plan a project once the immediate threat has receded. Daily life offers ample evidence that behaving only in response to pressure and fear is not the best way for living and making progress. In such a case, the major result is temporary survival in a fragile condition. If humankind is to be successful in establishing effective global governance, it will be the result of a proactive and deliberate choice by individuals and organized societies.

For reasons explained in chapter 1, it could be argued that the 1992 Rio Conference on Development and Environment was precisely an attempt to move toward a new choice concerning how to define, design, and produce the wealth of the world and share it at the global level by taking into account the great diversity of needs, aspirations, and potential of the many different groups of countries and populations of the world. The Rio Conference will stand in history as the first example of global negotiation for a contract on global wealth.[2] The most comprehensive written agreement resulting from the Rio Conference is Agenda 21, which was signed by delegates from more than 130 states (including heads of state, representatives from industry, NGOs, and voluntary associations, and scientists). Despite its shortcomings, Agenda 21 is a prototype of a global contract of great symbolic and potential political relevance.[3]

A contract is a choice because the focus on commonly identified objectives comes at the end of a process of assessment by all concerned parties (with initial divergent interests) that the benefits of "going together" are greater than the inconveniences. The result will be a win-win game (compared with the win-lose game that characterizes the competitive metaphor). The mutual recognition between Israel and the PLO is a good example of a contract between enemies who came to admit after more than forty years of war that "living peacefully together" is more advantageous than pursuing a devastating military conflict. A contract is the appropriate choice when the parties involved are numerous, the problems are complex and multidimensional, and the solutions are of a long-term structural nature. In fact, when a contract is signed after a long period of intensive and fair negotiations, it will mean that people have learned to mediate and develop an understanding of the other parties' viewpoints and interests.[4] A plan elaborated by a narrow group of world decisionmakers will have significantly less impact and receive less acceptance for a much shorter period of time than a plan that has been elaborated with the greatest possible involvement of people and signed by all concerned parties. The following are two examples of global contracts that imply processes that could lead to effective forms of global governance.

One of the most challenging and epoch-making contracts would be a pact among the religions of the world, although present trends are not very encouraging; the tendency seems to be for religious conflicts to expand in frequency, location, and intensity. (As mentioned in chapter 2, some people are convinced that the next global war will be caused by an unavoidable confrontation between what they call the Western and Islamic civilizations, but this forecast is founded on a caricature of current phenomena.) The many initiatives that have been promoted and implemented over the last twenty years at the global, regional, national, and city levels, with a view to establishing a dialogue among the various religions on a robust organizational basis, are encouraging. Their effects will be made more relevant, substantial, and durable by a new contract at the global level, complemented by a series of local protocols.[5]

Another significant contract would be one involving the citizens of several large and small cities of the world, major private foundations from the countries of the involved cities, and firms concerning the reorganization of urban transport systems. For even well-conceived and well-funded action at the level of a city acting alone would yield only limited results. Potential achievements will remain partial and unsatisfactory, and may even come with undesired perverse effects. Conversely, a multicity urban transportation deal would have a major impact on an extended search at the global level for innovative and effective solutions.

## Words Are Not Enough: Global Cooperative Governance Implies Clear Operational Targets

The risk in discussing the details of the contract is that one may lose sight of the overarching visions and objectives of the process. What exactly is the meaning of a contract with a view to easing the transition toward effective global governance? What does effective global governance mean in concrete terms?

Effective global governance is a system that, governed by people and institutions according to commonly defined rules and mechanisms, assures that all involved parties contribute to, and benefit from:

- efficient and environmentally sound use of available and potential natural and artificial resources (that is, an efficient world economy);
- extensive forms of accountable social solidarity between existing and future generations and different groups (that is, universal social justice);

• a dynamic and multivaried framework for the promotion and development of cultural identity, dialogue, and integration (that is, genuine cultural diversity and freedom);

• the largest possible participation of individuals and groups in the decisionmaking process, based on a pluralist and public-interest-inspired information and communication system (that is, advanced forms of political democracy).

As such, the definition given may be considered abstract. In reality, the definition underlines the magnitude of changes involved, and the time and resources needed, to establish an effective global governance.

Global governance demands energetic commitments over lengthy periods of time because the challenge facing the promotion of effective global governance is twofold. How can new socioeconomic and political spaces be organized at the world level, within the context of which nation-states will lose a degree of sovereignty in exchange for new forms of free representative and participatory democratic institutions? And how can free and rapidly expanding global capitalism be inserted into a socially, environmentally, and politically accountable system to benefit all citizens of the world? A possible response to the dual challenge is to choose the basic needs and aspirations of the world population as the primary target of global governance. By so doing, the principal function of a global contract is to contribute to the definition of these basic needs and aspirations, and to the selection of the resources to meet them. They are measurable and can be translated into specific operational targets. They belong to two main groups:

• the needs of existence, on a physical, socioeconomic, political, and cultural level. Existence demands that the world populations have access to:

| | |
|---|---|
| food | education |
| energy | freedom |
| shelter | security |
| health | work |

• the needs of coexistence, by means of physical and social infrastructures, socioeconomic rules and mechanisms, institutionalized forms of governance, and multiple forms of cultural dialogue. Coexistence demands that world populations have access to:

| | |
|---|---|
| transport | democracy |
| information | cultural identity |
| communication | justice |
| arts | solidarity |

As examples of such needs, we will describe shelter and communication. The scope and nature of the shelter need can be defined in concrete operational terms as follows:

- approximately 110 million people can be classified as homeless (approximately 10 million in North America and Western Europe; reliable data concerning the former Soviet Union and Central and Eastern Europe are not available);
- up to 1.5 billion people live in housing unworthy of that name;
- up to 2.5 billion people live in housing that is qualitatively inadequate from a material and socioeconomic perspective.[6]

What has to be done is known. The most urgent concrete objective is to provide housing for 1.5 billion people in the poorest regions of the world and to reurbanize the immense peripheries that are the manifestation of the urban maldevelopment in the richest regions of the world. The key issue is how to achieve the objective within a reasonable period of time—say a generation. Who is going to take a coordinated initiative at the regional and local level? Why are existing reasonable proposals from specialized United Nations agencies and regional and national organizations not implemented?[7] Who will finance the huge costs of acquiring the necessary land and establishing the basic infrastructures? How can self-help and self-management at the family and community levels be promoted and supported?

The case of communication is also definable in very concrete operational terms. Reduced to its simplest formulation, the communication need at the world level is how to give access to a telephone to half of the world's population, knowing for example that the area of Tokyo alone (24 million people) has more telephone lines than all of Africa (500 million people), and that Japan (110 million inhabitants) has more telephones than the developing countries of Asia, Africa, and South America put together (about 3 billion people).[8] Of course, the communication need embraces many other aspects that go beyond access to material infrastructures and technology. There is, for instance, a growing concern with regard to cultural identity and political democracy. The concern regards the present development of the mass media and its reorganization and consolidation at the world level (especially of newspapers and television) within and by a limited number of global consortia and networks.

It is to be hoped that constructive solutions at the world level will result from the still pending debate on whether the GATT regulations should be applied to cultural activities. In fact, the development and use of new information and communication technologies are affecting all forms of cultural expression. Cultural activities are increasingly designed, produced, distributed, and consumed in the same way as traditional industrial products and services. Hence there are those who think that cultural activities based on the new communication media are industrial products and services like any other and should be submitted to the same GATT rules. In the view of many others, cultural activities cannot be reduced to industrial goods and services. One has to preserve the diversity of cultures and avoid the financial and economic superiority of a country or a group of countries in the area of communication and information media, which might lead to the marginalization and ultimate disappearance of the cultures of economically weak countries and regions.[9] In this case, the "what to do" is still open to different solutions. How to find the way(s) to reach the solution(s) that will best respond to the needs and aspirations of the largest segment of the world population remains, again, the major issue.

## Growth of Noncompetitive Regimes

### The Regionalization Approach

The regionalization approach is based on the idea that it is easier and more effective to begin by integrating into an economic entity those countries of the same area that share a long history, traditions, and common values and are linked by proximity, rather than to try to bring together all countries and peoples of the world at once.

In many cases, this approach is also inspired by the functionalist principle, which says that the integration process among different states, peoples, and cultures must be a gradual one that moves first from creating a robust solidarity of economic interests among the parties of the concerned area, and then to building up the other forms of integration in the monetary, foreign affairs, and defense areas. The functionalist principle claims that this step-by-step process will ultimately lead to full political integration.

Regionalization processes have been taking place since the 1950s, in the form of the gradual elimination of all economic barriers that fragment regions into many national markets. Various examples of regionalization exist along a spectrum that ranges from a simple customs union to economic integration based on a monetary union and common economic policies, and on to the creation of a single integrated market or other forms of market integration and economic cooperation.

As shown in table 4.1, the majority of existing cases of regional economic integration are situated closer to the customs union model and to various forms of liberalization of national markets (often limited to the free circulation of goods and, in the case of the European Community only, encompassing the free circulation of capital, services, and people). The most advanced example of regional economic integration is the European Community, renamed the European Union on November 1, 1993. It is also the oldest one. The great majority of the other examples dates back only to the last five to ten years (see table 4.1).

No single example of a regional economic unit is truly comparable to others. Even if several examples belong to the category of customs unions, there are many relevant differences involving the size and importance of the countries involved in the union, the ultimate aim (whether the customs union is the first step toward a deeper form of economic and monetary union), the length of the period agreed on for the realization of the union (five, ten, fifteen years), the type of institutions set up to govern the transition process and then the union (with or without parliamentary assembly).

Major differences can be found across the continents. In Europe, the regional integration process has had, from its beginning in 1951 with the creation of the European Coal and Steel Community (ECSC), a political character and commitment. The mobilizing idea was and still is the full political integration of European peoples and countries. The concept and target of European unity—the "United States of Europe"—is deeply rooted in the contemporary history and culture of Europe. In contrast, in both North America and Latin America, the regional units basically remain within the concept and target of establishing free trade areas.[10] They also are based on a multilateralization of bilateral agreements or unions. The same applies to Oceania. In Asia, and particularly East and Southeast Asia, the movement is characterized by a multiplicity of ad hoc forms of cooperation agreements supported by, or operating within, the context of bilateral treaties and under the umbrella of multilateral organizations.[11] There is, for the time being, no

Table 4.1
An overview of existing examples of regional economic units

| Regional area | Countries involved | Date of establishment |
|---|---|---|
| **Africa and Arab Countries** | | |
| • AM, Union of Arab Maghreb | Algeria, Libya, Morocco, Mauritania, Tunisia | 1989 |
| • CEUCA, Custom and Economic Union of Central Africa | Gabon, Congo, Central African Republic, Chad | 1964 |
| **Americas** | | |
| • NAFTA, North American Free Trade Area | Canada, United States, Mexico (aim: creation of a free trade area) | 1991 |
| • PAECA, Plan de Action para America Central | Guatemala, Honduras, El Salvador (aim: creation of a free trade area) | 1992 |
| • MCCA, Mercado Commun Centro America | Costa Rica, Guatemala, Honduras, El Salvador, Nicaragua (facing difficulties). These countries have signed a free trade treaty for 1996 with Mexico. | 1985 |
| • Andino Pact | Bolivia, Columbia, Equador, Peru, Venezuela, facing frequent changes since its creation | 1964 |
| • MERCOSUR | Brazil, Argentina, Paraguay, Uruguay Barbados, Guyana, Jamaica | 1991 |
| • MCC, Mercado Commun Central | | |
| • ALADI, Latin American Organization for Integration | MERCOSUR + Andino Pact + Mexico (a series of bilateral and multilateral agreements), | 1980 |
| **Asia and Pacific** | | |
| • ASEAN, Association of South East Asian Nations | Brunei, Indonesia, Malaysia, Philippines, Singapore, Thailand | 1967 |

**Table 4.1** (*continued*)

| Regional area | Countries involved | Date of establishment |
|---|---|---|
| ● AFTA, Asian Free Trade Association | The ASEAN countries decided to create a Free Trade Area by 2008 | 1992 |
| ● SAARC, South East Asian Association for Regional Cooperation | India, Pakistan, Bangladesh, Bhutan, Sri Lanka, Maldives | 1985 |
| ● EAEC, East Asia Economic Council | ASEAN countries plus Japan, China, Taiwan, Hong Kong, South Korea | 1990 |
| ● APEC, Asia and Pacific Economic Cooperation | ASEAN countries plus Japan, USA, Canada, New Zealand, Australia, South Korea, Taiwan, Hong Kong, China | 1989 |
| ● OECCA, Organization for Economic Cooperation in Central Asia | Azerbaijan, Turkmenistan, Ouzbekistan, Kirchistan, Tadjikistan, Pakistan, Iran, Turkey | |
| **Europe** | | |
| ● EC, European Community | Federal Republic of Germany, Belgium, France, Italy, Luxembourg, the Netherlands, Denmark, Ireland, United Kingdom, Greece, Portugal, Spain | |
| ● EFTA, European Free Trade Area | Austria, Norway, Sweden, Switzerland, Iceland, Finland | |
| ● EEA, Economic European Area | EC countries plus EFTA countries | 1992 |
| ● CIS, Confederation of Independent States | Former Soviet Union countries | 1991 |
| ● ECABS, Economic Cooperation Area of Black Sea countries | Russia, Ukraine, Bulgaria, Rumania, Turkey, Greece, Armenia, Azerbaijan, | 1992 |

genuine free trade, customs, and economic union. The African and Arab countries are also characterized by a near absence of effective regional economic units. However, unlike Asia, they have experienced a regression process, as compared to the situation in the 1960s and 1970s, which was marked by the mushrooming of initiatives that gave birth to many treaties and institutions of economic integration. Most of them still exist, but only on paper.

The multiplicity and diversity of the examples of units of economic co-operation or institutions at the regional level does not allow firm conclusions to be drawn. It is even more difficult to make propositions concerning possible future developments. A few facts, however, can be underlined.

Leaders from all regions of the world give the impression that, although they are primarily led by the principle and imperative of competitiveness, they are conscious of the fact that the future well-being and development of their countries will also depend on greater cooperation with other countries in their region. Although in most cases regional free trade areas and customs unions are viewed as necessary and powerful instruments to increase a region's competitiveness vis-à-vis the other economic regions of the world, they also seem convinced that the process of regional integration is a vital condition for peaceful and balanced governance of the world economy.

Regional political integration today is nonexistent, with the unique exception of the European Community countries. It can therefore be said with a high degree of plausibility that if present trends continue for the next fifteen to twenty years, the development of regional integrated political unions will be slow and modest. If this happens, the effectiveness of the regionalization approach as a way of ensuring cooperative governance of the world economy could be significantly affected. Yet the example of the European Community could stimulate similar processes of integration elsewhere, particularly in Africa and Latin America. The intensity of the processes of political regional integration is of critical importance.

Interestingly, the regionalization approach remains, for the time being, limited to the economic sphere. Because of its basic inspiring principle—that is, the functionalist principle—the regionalized integrated world presupposes that effective global governance will emerge from a regionally based cooperative economic reorganization of the present globalizing economy.

The connection between the globalizing economy and the need for globalizing political governance, rules, and institutions is solved by assuming that the move toward a postnational state and postnational era of capitalism will lead to the creation of regional federations, and that institutionalized agreements among these regional entities will ensure global political governance.

On the other hand, the forty-year process of European integration proves that true economic and political regional integration takes time and represents the ingenuity, political will, and wisdom of several generations. In discussing the importance of the role of regionalization as a way of achieving an effective system of global governance within the context of the regionalized integrated world scenario, one must therefore take a long-term view. In this sense, no one can predict what the regional integration process in Central Asia, North Africa, Central America, or South Asia will look like in 2010 or 2020. Advanced forms of economic and political integration such as those achieved by the European Community countries seem simply unrealistic in these regions for the next ten to fifteen years. The move toward regional integration is a very recent phenomenon stimulated by the financial, trade, and economic globalization described in chapters 1 and 2.

Two philosophies will inspire and determine the fate of the regionalization approach in the next twenty years and its role in ensuring improved global governance. The first philosophy is represented by the prevalent market economic conception and opportunism. In most cases, regional integration (that is, customs union, market union, economic and monetary union) is considered to be a priority primarily with a view to achieving and maintaining an improved level of competitiveness of the countries of the regions in the globalizing economy.

If this philosophy should prevail in inspiring the move toward greater integration in all regions of the world, one may express some doubts about the positive contribution to a cooperative global governance that could be associated with the regionalization approach. In fact, replacing a nation-to-nation competitive economic war by a regional bloc-to-bloc competition for global leadership cannot be seen per se as a positive step. The risk of global domination by one or two blocs and division of the world between the integrated regions and the excluded regions will be very high. One argument in favor of the positive contribution that bloc-to-bloc competition is considered to make to global stability is that the cold war was based on the fight for

global supremacy between two world superpowers, and this struggle para-
doxically ensured a high level of world stability for at least thirty years. It
inhibited the explosion of a world war and thus contributed to a long period
of world economic growth until the 1970s. Hence the argument that it is
easier to manage economic "wars" among a small group of regions of the
world than economic wars among hundreds of countries of uneven size and
strength. Though understandable, the argument of the lesser evil remains
unsatisfactory, especially as a basis for a prescription for the future.

The second philosophy is represented by a constructive social and political
conception of codevelopment. This philosophy posits that institutional
forms of democratic codevelopment among different peoples, nations, and
communities of the same region constitute a powerful instrument for increasing the efficient allocation of available economic resources, thus improving the capability of the member countries' governments to promote
social welfare. Without a doubt, the situation in Africa would have been far
better if some form of African unity had been implemented. The future
would also look more promising if extreme fragmentation were replaced by
subregional and pan-African types of cooperative organizations. The same
applies to Latin America or Central Asia.

As already mentioned, the ideology of competitiveness and the corre-
sponding process of delinking between the most developed and the poorest
cities, regions, and countries of the world constitute severe obstacles to the
emergence of regionaly integrated units in the less-developed regions. There
is no real alternative, however, for these categories of regions than regional
integration within the context of a cooperative global framework. The
regionalization approach for codevelopment represents a crucial opportunity for common learning in the area of political democracy, pluralist government, effective economic management, social solidarity, and cultural
coexistence.

It would therefore be unjust to undermine the importance of the regionalization approach purely on the basis of an assessment of past or ongoing
events. There are reasonable grounds for believing that the regionalization
approach will expand in the future and emerge as the predominant form of
organization of the new global world.

## The Global Approach

The aim of adjusting the still nationally based political governance of world politics and society to the rapidly growing globalizing economy also lies at the basis of the global approach. Globalization is inspired by the need to reconcile politics, economics, and social justice by establishing rules, procedures, and institutions of political governance at the same level as that on which the global economy is operating.

Many ideas, goals, and perspectives coexist under the umbrella of the global approach. The cultural and sociopolitical matrix of the global approach is in fact highly diversified, because the principles and objectives of this approach originate from different social and interest groups. Thus the global approach encompasses meanings that in some instances are incompatible.

Supporters of the global approach are the globalizing enlightened elites from the richest, most developed, and leading countries of the world. Of course, these elites are internally divided by cultural differences and divergent economic and political interests. Generally speaking, however, they exhibit a remarkably coherent vision of globalization. Their most important contribution to the global approach is the support they give to all those elements that can contribute to strengthening economic, political, and cultural integration at the global level against the forces that can foster disintegration and hence impede the construction of the new global order. In doing so, the notions of integration/disintegration and the assessment of the relevant positive/negative factors are interpreted in line with their own values and interests. One of the leitmotifs of the globalizing enlightened elites is their insistence on the need for the establishment of the transnational conditions and mechanisms that will advance the governance of the global commons. They continually insist on global cooperation, necessitated by the acceleration of economic and technological development and by the new conditions for military and demographic security.[12] The participation of the elites in the promotion of the global approach raises the problem of consistency with the ideology of competitiveness, which they also strongly defend. The contradiction between the priority given to competitiveness as a goal and, at the same time, the support for a global approach is evident. One may argue that the contradiction is only apparent and that it is solved by the fact that, in the minds of the enlightened elites, the global approach is only instrumental and subordinated to the principle of competitiveness and to its preservation as the priority goal.

Another important contribution comes from what one may call the "In-Charge-of-the-World-Common-Interest-Organizations" (the "IWCIO"), that is, the part of the global civil society represented by those people, principles, processes, and institutions that are made by and exist around the multicomposite family of the United Nations system. Members of the IWCIO already have fifty years of experience,and they have played a major determining role in the design, development, and support of noncompetitive regimes in almost all areas of human activity. Be it education, science and culture (UNESCO), food and agriculture (FAO), employment and labor (ILO), industry (UNIDO), population (UNDP), migration, refugees, and health (WHO), the environment (UNEP), or trade and development (UNCTAD), the United Nations organizations—as well as the semipublic and professional organizations such as the International Telecommunication Union (ITU), the International Geographical Union (IGU), the International Science Council Union (ISCU), etc.—have significantly contributed to the emergence and strengthening of a global sensibility. Particularly in recent years, thanks to the Brandt Commission on development, the Palme Commission on security, the Brundtland Commission on environment and development, and Nyerere's South Commission, the members of the IWCIO have accepted the principles of global interdependence and the urgency of global cooperation. One should also note the important contribution made by the IWCIO since the 1970s to the definition and the implementation (though with rather limited success) of the so-called New International Economic Order (NIEO).[13]

The United Nations has recently created a new commission, the Global Cooperation Commission, whose goal is to submit for adoption by the fiftieth General Assembly of the United Nations in 1995—on the fiftieth anniversary of its founding—a revised charter of the United Nations organization with a view to increasing the conditions and mechanisms necessary for more effective democratic global cooperation and governance. In the context of the anniversary celebration, many proposals for some type of global government will probably be submitted for public debate. As one may reasonably anticipate, the response of governments—the states—that are the key decisionmakers in the UN system will be rather marked by reservations about proposals of radical innovation. Nevertheless, it is important that the celebration becomes an opportunity for building new stepping stones on the path toward an effective and democratic global governance.

It is not out of the question that within the decade events could bring us closer, for instance, to proposals for strengthening the global approach put forward by Vice President Al Gore in his manifesto *Earth in the Balance: Forging a New Common Purpose*.[14] Though the main thrust of Gore's book is the restoration of the balance now missing in humankind's relationship to the earth, the message derived from the chapter "A New Common Purpose" and " A Global Marshall Plan" is twofold. First, "there is no real precedent for the kind of global response now required,"[15] which means that readers are invited to recognize that humankind has entered a new era—of the globalization of human affairs—that demands global governance. Second, there is an urgent need to design and implement a plan that formalizes worldwide cooperation, a sort of global Marshall Plan. The new plan will require the wealthy nations to allocate money for transferring environmentally friendly technologies to the developing world and to aid impoverished nations in achieving stable population growth and new patterns of sustainable economic progress. To this end, "action should be taken within a framework of global agreements that obligates all nations to act in concert as part of an overall design focused on deriving a healthier and more balanced pattern in world civilization that integrates the Third World with the global economy."[16] To implement the global Marshall Plan, a world unit is, in Gore's view, neither feasible nor desirable. The most practical system for world governance would be negotiating international agreements that establish constraints on behavior.

The same concern inspired the conclusions in the 1992 report "Towards a New Global Design," prepared by the Japan Economic Research Institute.[17] The report emphasizes a new global design aimed at peace and harmony, democracy, freedom, and tolerance based on three processes:

● *a multilevel network system* based on the overall principles of subsidiarity and tolerance, and implying that decisionmaking power should be placed at the lowest efficient level; for many nations this means decentralization, and in other cases it may mean a supranational grouping; a decisionmaking space has to be established for small regions within states or for municipalities and towns; new forms of transborder networks should establish new supranational ties;

- *a world organization*, also based on the principle that some decisions requires a world view, that there is a form of world sovereignty above nations and groups of nations. A world organization implies both a transformation of some aims of existing international organizations (for the promotion of policies like fixed exchange rates, free movement of goods, services, and factors of production, and mutual recognition of operational systems) and the creation of new world institutions to deal directly with world issues (energy and nonrenewable resources, environmental protection, space exploration, and ocean management). At a certain point in time, world organizations should operate with independent funding (oil or $CO_2$ taxes, direct taxation on high-income groups, or on transnational corporations with world legal status);
- *a social contract* for the management of North-South relations, including a world employment policy, some form of income redistribution, and a generalization of social protection (insurance, health) and equal opportunity (education).

The move toward a global social contract could be considered the main objective of the third group of people, principles, and organizations that contributes to the global approach. We refer to the other members of global civil society, the nature and role of which was discussed in chapter 1.

The most active members of the global civil society are those who strongly believe in the concept of one planet and the absolute priority of the global common good and their maintenance and expansion by means of adequately empowered global institutions. They advocate actively in favor of the recognition of a world citizenship, a world government, and a world democracy. One finds within this group the many voluntary associations and NGOs that work on so-called alternative development.[18] Taken together, they regroup millions of people.

The various promoters of the global approach may have opposing views and may defend conflicting interests. They contribute, however, in an unplanned and uncoordinated manner, giving credibility, legitimization, and strength to the global approach.

Though the idea of global governance based on tacit and explicit international agreements that will contribute to the design and development of a global social contract may appear unrealistic, the preceding discussion suggests that a global social contract will not emerge from a response to urgent global problems. It will result from the combined effect of uncoordinated choices and actions of thousands of organizations throughout the world that share a common perception and consciousness of the new global world era.

## The Next Step: Four Global Social Contracts

The world has become one, woven by interlocking economies, ideologies, migrations, environmental issues, and communications. This one world is characterized by

1. uncertainty, whether political, economic (threat of job loss), or technological (high rate of obsolescence); urgency, because many seemingly irreversible situations loom large; and necessity, because a high concentration of poverty and degradation creates survival mentality;

2. reactions in the face of the unknown that can lead to uncontrolled situations such as social intolerance, nationalism, and excessive competition;

3. new actors, that is, the loose network of NGOs, the scientific community (because of environmental and bioethical issues) ; the media, the new governance complex (G7, European Union, United Nation organizations); emerging economic powers of Southeast Asia;

4. a sense of difficult adaptation in critical areas such as education, work, social programs, ethnic relations, development, and management.

Cooperative global governance is about facing these issues and managing to agree on some shared directions, not only to avoid dangers (such as nuclear peril, widespread conventional armed conflicts, environmental catastrophes), but also to progress toward increased material and nonmaterial wealth in the general interest of the growing world population.

To achieve such proactive intervention of citizens and communities, it is necessary

1. to agree on some basic principles; and

2. to establish new global contracts based on the deliberate choices of all of the concerned actors, being aware of the necessity of acting with a sense of urgency but also with a long-term perspective (one generation at least) and with a sense of priorities while encouraging changes in modes and means of governance.

**Principles and Operation**

To progress toward effective global governance, it is imperative to elaborate a set of principles. These are:

• The instruments we use must be cooperative. This is the condition necessary to ensure the principle of efficiency. While economic competition is not capable by itself of attaining adequate human development in global society, collaborative processes—implying exchange, sharing, negotiations, common purposes—are not only instruments of betterment for human beings and the condition for long-term security and development of humanity, but also contribute to democratic purposes and progress. Cooperation can make better use of resources and ensure confidence and efficiency.

• Global civil society must be supported. The many different types of organizations and social groups that make up global civil society represent a powerful tool of democratic dynamics: they can bring visibility to issues, force accountability, bring precision to public decisionmaking and, sometimes, are the very basis for the emergence of democratic structures. This principle postulates a vitality among the new actors; it entails respect for the principle of responsibility, and the commitment to giving, and sharing responsibility.

• As a corollary to the principle of responsibility, local actions, behaviors, and experiments that respond to the new paradigm of globalization must be systematically recognized and supported at the global level. This is the principle of relevance. A vast and fertile field of creativity remains unexploited, while attention is given to banal, standardized, but highly marketable needs, goods, and services that are not of direct relevance to the largest number of humans. Imaginative collaborations have to be deployed by transnational corporations, the bureaucracy of the United Nations, regional organizations, and the NGO community to connect innovative local actions. It is time to reduce the waste of innovative potential.

• Cultural diversity has to be explicitly integrated into our ways of thinking and acting. The unease surrounding immigration in many countries, the resurgence of ethnocentric rhetoric and behaviors, the social tensions arising out of confrontations among racial groups in large cities across the world, and the capacity for religious adherence to spearhead political activities leading to violence all indicate the necessity for the global society we have created to explicitly address cultural diversity. It is essential to recognize this diversity as a challenge to communicate and share rather than to compete.

Based on these principles, we must chart change that takes into account the issues, challenges, and opportunities previously analyzed. Proposals for action are thus devised under the name "common endeavors." They are based upon the idea that the global society and, in particular, the satisfaction of the basic needs and aspirations of the 8 billion people who will inhabit the planet by 2020 should be the primary target of the visions, strategies, and actions of humankind. Thus common endeavors start with four global contracts (see figure 4.1). Promoting human and social development on a global scale requires:

- sustaining basic needs and aspirations;
- assuring mutual recognition and fruitful exchanges between cultures;
- building instruments of global governance;
- adequately preserving environmental resources.

Global contracting means the identification and promotion of principles, institutional modalities, financial mechanisms, and practices that allow the allocation of material and nonmaterial resources in the general interest of world society, in particular, for the satisfaction of the basic needs of the poorest populations. The aim of each contract is to stimulate the growth of world wealth in the most sustainable manner from a human, social, economic, environmental, and political perspective.

According to the most recent reports from the United Nations Development Program and the World Bank, the poorest populations of the world share 5.6 percent of the world income and represent 3.5 billion people. In addition, according to local official data, there are 53 million poor people in the United States and 40 million in the European Community countries, not to mention approximately 80–100 million in Eastern Europe and the former Soviet Union.

The global contracts—in a tacit or explicit form—are destined to identify and promote those principles, institutional modalities, financial mechanisms, and practices that will make it possible to satisfy the basic needs of more than 3.7 billion people in the coming twenty to thirty years.

### The First Contract: The Contract for Basic Needs (Removing Inequalities)
Relieving the poorest populations of the world is not an unrealistic target. To provide housing to the 30 million homeless in the United States and Western

Principles

> • The instruments we use must be collaborative (principle of efficiency).
>
> • Global civil society must be supported, encouraged, and accounted for (principle of responsibility).
>
> • Local actions and experiences should be systematically recognized (principle of relevance).
>
> • Cultural diversity has to be explicitly acknowledged (principle of universal tolerance).

Common endeavors: Four global contracts

| | |
|---|---|
| The Having Contract "Remove inequality" | The Cultural Contract "Tolerance and dialogue of cultures" |
| The Democratic Contract "Toward global governance" | The Earth Contract "Implement sustainable development" |

Direction

> A new sense of belonging "beyond conquest"

**Figure 4.1**
Charting change

Europe or to the expanding army of homeless in Russia is possible. The same applies to the millions of homeless in the rest of the world. The object of this contract is:

- water, for 2 billion people;
- shelter, for 1.5 billion people;
- efficient energy, for 4 billion people.

The components of the contract would be developed through a series of agreements between private firms, governmental agencies, financial institutions, and foundations. It implies close cooperation among private enterprises, public authorities, financial institutions, and voluntary associations from both the developed and the developing countries. Each agreement should address a specific number of jointly determined actions aimed at enhancing local and global skills, capital, infrastructure, and institutions for the promotion of social development industries.

Regarding instruments for implementation, the original stimulus should come from the people of the three most developed regions of the world, in the form of a joint resolution by the Japanese Diet and other Asian parliaments, the European parliament, the U.S. Congress, and the Canadian and Mexican parliaments. The resolution should commit the respective governments and invite concerned national and multinational firms as well as foundations and voluntary associations to set up the operational framework to guide the implementation, management, and assessment of actions relating to shelter, water, and energy. The resolution should also identify the means (financial, in particular) for defining a global pact among relevant national and multinational corporations, banks, national governments, and associations from the developed and developing countries. In the case of the development of water supply and distribution networks and the provision of basic energy, for instance, Hydro-Québec, la Lyonnaise des Eaux (France), l'Instituto Costaricano d'Electricidad, the Indian Water Board—to mention only a few corporations—should be involved, together with national and international authorities for energy and the environment, and grassroots movements.

The selected projects should receive the label of global partnerships. The firms prepared to enter the agreement would, in turn, receive the global partner label, which would entitle them to long-term privileges (fiscal immunity, tax reduction, employment facilitation, information access) attached to the implementation of the agreement.

As for the desired consequences, among the anticipated results would be the massive construction of infrastructure, promotion of local capacity, and use of local material—all major steps toward a new technological basis for sustainable development.

Regarding water, some data helps to illustrate the problem and its urgency, and to delineate some major directions for action:[19]

- diarrheal diseases that result from contaminated water kill about 2 million children and cause some 900 million illnesses each year;
- 1 billion people lack access to safe water, while in the state of California alone (with 25 million inhabitants) there are 600,000 swimming pools;
- some 300 million people in urban areas and 1.3 billion in rural areas have no access to sanitation;
- fish stocks are rapidly declining as a result of water pollution;
- aquifer depletion is leading to irreversible damage.

Water pollution and water scarcity demand immediate attention. Action should be taken along several lines at once: steps to confront local or national problems in developed countries (such as desalinization and water-saving measures); provision of safe water in the large urban agglomerations; joint action between developed and developing countries (for example, reducing oceanic pollution). Most of the very practical and effective measures that should be taken are already detailed in Agenda 21. Groups of private and public corporations and foundations should promote the organization of a joint planning conference, during which a memorandum of understanding and a plan for providing safe water for 2 billion people could be discussed and submitted for joint financing by the World Bank and regional banks.

Regarding shelter, the combination of identified and implemented top-down and bottom-up projects will lead to an effective use of local materials, involving local communities and the application of higher technologies in hybrid ways. Equally, priority should be given to actions that would minimize costs.

In the developed countries, where the most critical problem is social exclusion, priority should be given to the restructuring of declining city centers, dedicating reconverted areas to housing targeted to young couples, the elderly, and immigrants from the developing countries. The construction of shelters by future occupants should be strongly encouraged. This could be done through nongovernmental organizations that have the scope to intervene in habitat improvement processes. This would make it easier to introduce basic racial and social integration.

### The Second Contract: The Cultural Contract
### (Tolerance and Dialogue of Cultures)

The object of this contract is the support of policies and campaigns to promote tolerance and dialogue among cultures. The contract would be designed and promoted through a series of events based, among others things, on the extensive use of advanced information and communication technologies and of public places (schools, theaters, museums).

Instruments for implementation include all institutions, private and public, throughout the world that can provide a consistent forum for cultural initiatives. Our proposal is that a limited number of cities (forty to fifty) from all regions of the world, together with local media firms and voluntary associations, with the support from national and international foundations, sponsor a series of educational campaigns on the model of the initiative taken by Belgium called Europalia. These campaigns would promote awareness and cooperation at the world level through exhibitions, concerts, movies, joint TV programs with press coverage, etc., every two to three weeks on different cultures of the world and their interaction with other cultures, cultural problems, and prospects. Large corporations such as Time Warner, Bertelsman, Bell Atlantic, and TCI should be invited to sponsor programs and debates on various aspects of religion, culture, and history on a bimonthly worldwide basis. Similarly, international networks of universities should launch six-month student foreign exchange programs (with targets of a thousand students per year for the first three years).

Finally, a group of smaller countries along with a collection of nongovernmental organizations should produce a yearly report on the dialogue of cultures, comparable to the report of the United Nations Development Program on Human Development.

As a consequence, the dialogue of cultures should become a modus operandi for the implementation of the three other contracts, as well as constituting one of their explicit objectives. Maximizing the dialogue via a multiplicity of modes is a most effective road to a new global world and to the global contracts.

## The Third Contract: The Democratic Contract
## (Toward Global Governance)

This contract is of fundamental importance. Its relevance and urgency derive from what we have called the fundamental weakness of present globalization, that is, the increasing dissociation between economic power organized on a world basis by global networks of industrial, financial, and service enterprises, and political power that remains organized at the national level only. Under these circumstances, the more national public authorities consider it the principal task of the state to ensure that their own multinational companies (the only ones armed to act within the world economy) are or become competitive in international and global markets, the more the state assigns these companies the task of defending and promoting the economic and social well-being of the country. In so doing, such corporations are given the legitimacy needed to ensure the optimal worldwide management of global material and nonmaterial resources. The result is that representative democratic mechanisms do not operate at a global level. The global system is led instead by oligarchical power structures that tend to merge into more efficient and integrated networks, bypassing nation-state governments.

If the present trend continues, the world will be governed not only in the economic sphere but in other spheres as well by a group of private networks of stateless and unaccountable firms. These networks will generate new forms of political authority, legitimacy, and control that will have little in common with what we are used to calling democracy. The object of this contract is to contribute to reversing the trend. It will be particularly difficult to do so, but it is an unavoidable imperative.

The main component would be a campaign in support of the establishment of a global citizens assembly by the year 2000. The assembly should be convened the first time by an ad hoc interparliamentary session of national legislative bodies, with the support of the United Nations General Assembly. An international parliamentary association would act as a forum for almost all parliaments of the world. Its immediate task would be to reassess and define the elements, conditions, and objectives of what should become in the third millennium a new citizenship. Such new citizenship would provide constructive prescriptions about global commonality in terms of economic goods and properties and would focus on the practical implementation of the new frameworks for cooperative economic governance as alternatives for competitive frameworks. A global citizens assembly would constitute the representation of the transnational/global civilian society, which has been growing in the last thirty years at local, continental, and international levels and will continue to expand in the twenty-first century.

More than fifty years after the founding of the United Nations, an organization that adequately reflected the intergovernmental and international characteristics of the world at that time, the acceleration of history makes it a necessity to establish new forms of common institutions for that reflect the growing transnational and global character of today's world.

The global citizens assembly should gradually lead to the transformation of the United Nations General Assembly into a senate of the world, where national and supranational governments will be represented. Embryonic examples of the global citizens assembly—although largely inadequate— exist in many areas. Their experiences could serve to help avoid mistakes and promote solutions that proved efficient and effective. The International Association of Cardiologists, for example, which convenes every four years for a one-week seminar, includes more than 4,000 specialists and is just one of dozens of associations capable of global exchange and management. The same applies to the World Council of Churches, whose 1,000 representatives meet for a month every two years. These examples show that the organization of an ad hoc world assembly representing millions of people, organized into national chapters, special committees and subcommittees, task forces, general world secretariats, and so on, is not only feasible but is an intrinsic necessity to any world system that wishes to survive.

The establishment of a global citizens assembly would be a major constructive step toward the imperative process of democratization of world society in at least two respects:

• it would offer the unique opportunity—that does not exist today—to formulate a global social demand resembling the one expressed on an ad hoc basis by the United Nations Conference on Environment and Development in Rio in 1992;

• it would also provide a second unique opportunity for the emergence and development of a new global political player that could act as the needed organizational mechanism for dialogue, negotiation, and partnership with the global private networks of multinational firms that govern today's economic world. If private interests primarily govern the world economy and society, there will be no buffer to deal with major conflicts, wars, maldevelopment, and social, economic, environmental, and cultural costs. Private global players need public global players (and vice-versa). The present international/intergovernmental institutions are not an adequate response, inasmuch as they do not reflect the supranational textures of private global actors.

To prevent the global citizens assembly from being transformed into a neatly justified political organization distanced from reality, several global networks should be strengthened or promoted. Several existing international networks among cities already play a positive role. They should be globalized, and their ability to carry out joint projects must be strengthened by concrete action (such as the water and shelter initiatives outlined above).

Second, a global network of scientific organizations is needed. There already exist a large number of very valuable international and world scientific associations. They are, however, much too fragmented and specialized. It is time for scientists and their professional organizations to learn to work together on ad hoc projects. Some such projects already exist, but it is necessary to increase the effectiveness with which scientific knowledge is used to advance the interests of the poorest populations of the world rather than merely bolster the competitiveness of the strongest and richest countries. This global network of scientific organizations should be one of the practical instruments of the world council of knowledge (see the next contract).

**The Fourth Contract: The Earth Contract (Sustainable Development)**
The final component of the policy for common endeavors is to accelerate the implementation of the commitments made by more than 130 governments at the 1992 Rio Conference on Environment and Development. Agenda 21 deals with both the pressing problems of today and the need to prepare for the challenges of the next century. It recognizes the responsibility of governments for the promotion of sustainable development, and it calls for the

broadest public participation in implementation and underlines the need for substantial new financial assistance for developing countries.

Agenda 21 addresses four major areas:

- social and economic dimensions;
- conservation and management of resources;
- strengthening the role of major groups;
- means of implementation.

It is accompanied by:

- a statement of principles on forests;
- a United Nations framework convention on climate change;
- a convention on biological diversity;
- a declaration covering all the above;
- a convention to fight desertification signed in 1994.

The range of issues addressed by Agenda 21 is so broad and fundamental (for example, combating poverty, changing consumption patterns, protecting and promoting human health, combating desertification, evolving sustainable agriculture and rural development, managing radioactive waste, enhancing the roles of children and youth in sustainable development, strengthening the role of farmers, reorienting business and industry) that the real issue is simply political will and operational choice.

A series of national action plans for sustainable development have been elaborated in accordance with Agenda 21. For its part, the United Nations has created groups to put into action the commitments made (in particular the ratification of the climate change and the biodiversity conventions). These are necessary basic actions.

One other essential component concerns business and industry. A Euro-American-Japanese roundtable of industrialists and bankers should be set up to encourage the world's largest 1,000 firms (and other willing firms) to sign a global contract on a common series of projects, selected from the areas covered by Agenda 21. These projects would receive financial support from the firms themselves as well as from international financial development agencies. Participation would entitle firms to use the "global partners" label. Unlike the national action plans, the twenty-first-century building projects taken on by the firms would be global by definition, though locally operated through global networks. (The 1,000 largest firms in the world are accustomed to networking and should not therefore be faced with a lack of experience.)

To implement Agenda 21 and the projects initiated by industrialists and bankers, an effort should be made to review and reform the international institutions that make up the Bretton Woods system (that is, the IMF and the World Bank). Set up after World War II, they celebrated their fiftieth anniversary in 1994.

One way to regenerate the world economic and financial frameworks is to transform the newly created World Trade Organization (WTO) into an interregional trade and cooperation organization. As mentioned in chapters 1 and 2, world economic development is no longer based on the exchange of goods among national economic entities interacting with each other according to the old scheme of an international division of labor, based on each nation's comparative advantage. The rapid growth of global cooperative networks and strategic alliances among multinational firms have made the global economy more of a home economy where firms, consumers, public authorities, and other nonprofit economic actors are increasingly taking part in the design, production, use, and recycling of common products, services, and processes.

Furthermore, as noted in chapters 2 and 4, the growing importance of regional economic integration and entities such as the European Community, NAFTA and Mercosur are challenging the principles of liberalization and deregulation on which the GATT dialogue was established. The new World Trade Organization can allow the creation of a larger unified market without a common external tariff, as in the case of NAFTA, or support a move toward global liberalization, as in the case of the European Community. What has become necessary is establishing new rules for active cooperation among the new regional economic entities and discouraging regional entities from becoming closed trade blocs competing against each other. As recent events have illustrated, the GATT is rather ineffective in preventing and stopping trade wars between blocs. In this respect, it does not seem that the WTO is better equipped than the GATT. New principles and modalities, based on cooperative frameworks rather than on conflicting liberalization and deregulation, have to be formulated and applied if the next century is not going to become a theater of major economic wars among world blocs.

**Box 4.1**
Meaning and feasibility of the global contract

The sequence of the elements analyzed in this section can be summarized as follows:
- The contract is an instrument leading to effective global governance.
- Effective global governance consists of four major ingredients: an efficient global economy, universal social justice, a genuine cultural identity and freedom, and an effective political democracy.
- These ingredients highlight the twofold challenge facing the move toward effective global governance (that is, the organization of entities beyond nation-%states and of a postnational capitalist world system).
- A response to the twofold challenge is to target the basic needs and aspirations of the world's population.
- The contract has to contribute to the least controversial definition possible of the basic needs and aspirations of the world's population, and to the identification of the most appropriate ways to cope with the twofold challenge.

The interregional trade and cooperation organization is one such possible framework. The development of more Lomé Convention-type agreements is another.

The regeneration of the world economy will also occur through the abandonment of the strategy of the IMF and World Bank based on the "three D's" of deflation, devaluation, and deregulation.[20] This prescription, which for decades has been the driving force of structural adjustment policies, has had severely debilitating effects on the poorer regions. Furthermore, not only have poorer nations incurred major ecological, social, and human disruptions, but rich nations have also been penalized. The restrictions and influence of the GATT, in combination with the structural adjustment policies and economic requirements of the IMF and the World Bank, have in fact ultimately contributed to global problems. To reverse the trend, the "three D's" should become the "three R's"—that is, recovery of mutual growth and trade, restructuring of the relations between public and private economic power, and redistribution of resources as a means of sustaining recovery.

Accordingly, new codevelopment networks should be created after the activities of the World Bank, IMF, WTO, UNDP, UNICEF, FAO, UNESCO, and ILO have been restructured and better integrated. Public organizations

**Box 4.2**
Some "enzymes" of the global approach

| | |
|---|---|
| Third World Network | International Federation for Alternative Trade |
| Development Alternative with Women for a New Era | Choosing Our Future |
| Helsinki Citizens Assembly | International Foundation for Development Alternatives |
| The Asian Council for People's Culture | World Association for World Federation |
| Conferences on a More Democratic United Nations | The International Organization of Consumers Unions |
| The World Order Models Project | Permanent People's Tribunal |
| Global Exchange | The European Civic Forum |
| ATD-Quart Monde | The International Body Food Action Network |
| Amnesty International | |
| Coordination Body for Indigenous Peoples' Organizations of the American Basin | African Network of Indigenous Environment and Development |
| Third World Forum | The Environment Liaison Centre International |
| International Association for Community Development and Action | The Global Citizens' Conference |
| The Friends of the Wilderness for Tropical Rainforest Campaign | The World Foundation for Deaf Children |
| The United Nations of Youth | Action for Rational Drugs in Asia |
| The International Popular Theater Alliance | The International Commission of Jurists |

have to be transformed immediately in order to enter the globalization process with maximum effectiveness.

The goal of reorganization of the World Bank and the IMF should be to eradicate the present hierarchical system in which the rich countries decide what is good for the poor countries. Conversely, it should promote the gradual development of a multiple, pluralistic type of network composed of decentralized (regional and transnational) agencies, based on effective forms of partnership among rich and poor countries. The codevelopment networks would act as a short-term investment fund and as a long-term development bank. They would promote and support a wide range of Lomé

Convention-type agreements or integrated projects, as well as labor-market development and employment-creation initiatives that are absent today on a global scale. They would be based on project task forces and public/private partnerships, with which would be linked not only international private and public financial and economic actors, but also nonprofit organizations (such as foundations) and voluntary associations. In this context, a decentralized agency should be a world council of knowledge. Its main aim would be to promote, via ad hoc private/public partnership projects, the use of existing knowledge and technologies and their improvement in such a way that:

• local ability for innovation is enhanced;
• local know-how and ingenuity can be exploited to address local basic needs in a constructive North-South development context, which does not introduce the usual negative constraints and requirements of the IMF, World Bank, and GATT/WTO;
• an effective cooperative transfer of knowledge in a South-South framework—as opposed to an unbalanced North-South relationship—could be stimulated, organized, and experienced.

The world council of knowledge would also have the task of involving from the outset of each project scientists, technologists, and business innovators—particularly from the poorer regions—in the development and implementation of new knowledge and technology. If such an integrated approach does not occur, the transfer of knowledge and technology will remain one-way (from the developed regions to the poorer ones) and will encounter more obstacles in the future. The "transplant" will be less and less possible because of the widening gap between the developed countries and the poorer regions in the design, development, appropriation, and use of the new knowledge and technologies.

Being (the democratic contract), having (the contract for meeting the basic needs of 3 billion people), living together (the earth contract), and relating (the cultural contract) are the key elements of working together for a global contract and cooperative governance.

It is suggested that an important role is to be played by cities, foundations, and other organizations from the civil society, in addition to, and in cooperation with, public authorities and private firms. Cities are particularly important because one major consequence of the globalization of technology, economy, and society is the reemergence of cities as key actors on the global scene. This is obvious not only for those large cities that already play a global role, such as New York, London, and Tokyo in the area of financial services,[21] Paris in cultural affairs, or Amsterdam, Copenhagen, Frankfurt, Zurich, Los Angeles, Osaka, Milan, San Francisco, Rome, Singapore, Hong Kong, Chicago, or Houston in a wide variety of sectors. Everywhere cities are increasingly developing new urban policies whose scope is, in most cases, determined without direct link to national governments. Increasingly numerous are the cities that take an active part in international and global networks. In many areas, cities can in fact offer a more open, flexible, and participatory framework than the nation-state in the design and implementation of collaborative projects. They can represent one of the building blocks of the new global world.

A philosopher from ancient Rome said, "The wind blows for those who know where they want to go." An even older Chinese maxim says, "Those who have thought too long before making any next step will remain all their lives on one foot." Very rarely do people deliberately choose to remain in this position.

# Conclusion: Hegemony Will Not Work

We have described the forces that link us all to a new global world, in particular through the increasing density of global communications that create common perceptions and profound patterns of interconnection.

We have reaffirmed the complexity of the world to which we belong in describing the globalization of the economy, the fragility of the ecosystem's capacity to support life, the new threats to political democracy at the global level, the might of scientific and technological potential, and the paucity of social justice and of cultural dialogue and tolerance.

Above all, we have analyzed the limits to competition and the paradoxical results that excessive competition can produce. We have shown that the imperative of economic competition cannot govern the planet and that the logic of conquest—of markets, of economic and financial power—is outdated and unrealistic. Accordingly, we have identified cooperative coexistence and governance as a realistic and effective route, and we have proposed the establishment of a new set of four global contracts.

At this point, however, many questions remain.

## Open Questions

Who will design the global contracts? Who will sign them? What makes us think that national governments, global networks of multinational firms, trade unions, local voluntary associations, ethnic groups, churches, universities, and the military will be ready to work on a cooperative basis for the satisfaction of the basic needs and aspirations of the world population, and poor people in particular?

Three social agents, we believe, will act in support of the conception, design, implementation, and promotion of the global contract idea and will become the explicit societal vehicles for the signature of the four suggested global contracts. These are: global civil society (including trade unions, if they succeed in converting themselves into more active global organizations based on new forms of local labor development); the global enlightened elites from industry, academia, government, media, and foundations acting within the context of new innovative cooperation schemes and systems of global multicultural, multinational, and multiterritorial governance (of particular relevance will be local forms of cooperative alliance between small and medium-sized companies, foundations, and urban authorities); and finally, the cities themselves, that is, the different social groups and institutions that focus on city development and government. As a matter of fact, cities have become increasingly subject to important policy choices in response to pressure from the globalization process as well as to the new wave of democratization and to their own development syndromes and problems.

The second open question is psychological. The celebration in 1992 of the five-hundredth anniversary of the "discovery" by Europeans of a new world made us aware that:

• This discovery deeply altered—not always for the better—the course of existence of millions of people and entire continents; in particular it paved the way for the emergence of a global world; it brought about new global values, such as the competition among nations for world domination. The need for creating colonial empires followed from the discovery. There is a kind of analogy and continuity between the new era of competition opened up by the discovery of the new world 500 years ago and the competitive era associated with the emergence of today's new global world. We now realize that we cannot repeat the same history for the next 500 years, for our accumulated power of destruction is so enormous that a repetition of past modes of behavior will lead to global destruction. The immediate and long-term future, therefore, cannot be marked by the same spirit of conquest of nature and domination of other peoples and nations. Are we as individuals, groups, organizations, nations, and regions ready to weaken the spirit of conquest and domination and enhance the spirit of cooperation and solidarity?

• In today's new global world three powerful entities (the United States, Western Europe, and Japan) share the governance of world politics, military power, and the economy. Within this context, Japan and more generally speaking the Southeast Asian region is considered to be the most dynamic. In the longer run, other Asian countries are approaching the level of a strong capacity to participate in the club of global powers. More important, we realize that the dominant actors are no longer countries but often transnational global firms that have lost, at least partly, identification with a clear nationality or national territory. To what extent are the global networks of multinational firms intrinsically able and willing to promote transparent and accountable global governance?

• The third open question is of a political nature. We have to recognize that our world has not arrived at the stage of a Kantian utopia (that is, universal peace). Rather, we live in a disintegrating world, characterized by a growing divide between the world of the peoples, cities, countries, and regions who "belong," in global power terms, and the world of the excluded peoples, cities, countries, and regions. The forces at work in favor of the global divide are the strongest because we still rely on old and ill-conceived ideas of economic competition and international globalization. Thus, to what extent will the people, cities, and regions of North America, Western Europe, Japan, and Southeast Asia enter into contracts, codetermined actions, and commitments to disseminate growth on all continents? In so doing, will they take into account the preservation of nature's resources and equity among the inhabitants of a planet rendered small by the population explosion, the technological and industrial apparatus, and shared aspirations across the globe for better human and social development? How is it possible to accelerate such a process and see to it that the cooperative pact is "signed" in the not-too-distant future?

### The Cooperative Pact

The path toward the implementation of the four global contracts that we have proposed will be long and difficult. The objectives of the global contracts, however, are realistic and achievable. To this end, the initiative for the adoption of the global contracts must come from Western Europe, North America, and Japan. Instead of using their enormous human, technological, and material resources, organizational expertise, and political power to compete for dominance in the twenty-first century, Japan, North America, and Western Europe will make the most fruitful, efficient, and noble use of their resources, expertise, and power by signing a cooperative pact. This pact of global cooperative governance would commit Western Europe, North America, and Japan to the following:

1. to plan the global social contracts;
2. to propose them to the other regions of the world with a view to starting a process for a new global agreement;
3. to identify the means to implement the four global contracts .

The representatives of civil society and the "enlightened elites" from Western Europe, North America, Japan, and the four newly industrialized countries should profit from the activities surrounding the fiftieth anniversary of the United Nations. Such events are the first steps of a process leading in the coming years to the definition, discussion, and implementation of the essential components of the global social contract for the twenty-first century.

# Notes

## Introduction: A Purposeful Planet

1. Cf. *Webster's Seventh New Collegiate Dictionary* (Springfield, MA: Merriam-Webster, 1969).

2. "Democracy is a political concept involving several dimensions: (1) contestation over policy and political competition for office; (2) participation of the citizenry through partisan, associational, and other forms of collective actions; (3) accountability of rulers to the rules through mechanisms of representation and the rule of law; and (4) civilian control over the military." From Terry Lynn Karl, "Dilemma of Democratisation in Latin America," in *Competitive Politics* 23, no. 1 (October 1990): 2. See also Philippe C. Schmitter and Terry Lynn Karl, "What Democracy Is . . . and Is Not," in *Journal of Democracy* 2, no. 3 (summer 1991): 75–88.

3. Riccardo Petrella, "L'Évangile de la Compétitivité," *Le Monde Diplomatique*, Paris, September 1991.

4. Cf. *A Competitive Strategy for America*, Second Report to the President and Congress, Competitiveness Policy Council, March 1993. The creation of a European Council of Competitiveness composed of industrialists, politicians, and scientists, with the exclusion of labor unionists, was the main proposal made in November 1993 in a document entitled *Beating the Crisis* transmitted to the president of the Commission of the European Union by the European Round Table of Industrialists (ERTI). The ERTI regroups the "patrons" of the seventeen largest European corporations. The gospel of competitiveness has no national borders.

5. See Terry L. Karl and Philippe C. Schmitter, "Democratization around the Globe: Opportunities and Risks," in *World Security: Challenges for a New Century*, 2d ed., ed. Michael T. Klare and Daniel C. Thomas (New York: St. Martin's Press, 1994).

6. Cf. Marshall McLuhan, *Understanding Media—The Technological Extension of Man* (New York: McGraw-Hill, 1964).

7. Armand Mattelart, *La Communication-Monde* (Paris: Editions La Découverte, 1992); Sean O'Siochru, *Global Sustainability, Telecommunications and Science and Technology Policy*, FAST, Commission of the European Communities, Brussels, 1993.

8. World Commission on Environment and Development, *Our Common Future* (Oxford: Oxford University Press, 1987).

9. Stephan Schmidheiny with the Business Council for Sustainable Development, *Changing Course—A Global Business Perspective on Development and the Environment* (Cambridge, MA: MIT Press, 1992).

10. The focus has been put on limits to competition rather than describing a world beyond competition or a postcompetitive world. Limits to competition clearly suggests that the members of the Group of Lisbon unanimously agree on one fact: strict competition has structural limits because it is unable to solve current problems of development throughout the world.

## Chapter 1

1. International Telecommunications Union, *The Missing Link*. Report of the Independent Commission on Worldwide Telecommunications Development (The Maitland Commission), Geneva, 1984.

2. Walther Richter, "Rural Telecommunications as a Vehicle for Growth." Paper presented at the International Telecommunications Futures Symposium, Omaha, Nebraska, 1991, p. 6.

3. George Muskens and Jacob Gruppelaar, eds., *Global Telecommunication Networks: Strategic Considerations* (Dordrecht, Boston, London: Kluwer Academic Publishers, 1988). For more recent information, see the Survey on Global Telecommunication by the Financial Times.

4. "A Scramble for Global Networks," *Business Week*, March 21, 1988.

5. The recent history of greatly overestimated forecasts about ISDN development and markets should invite people to adopt a more cautious attitude.

6. Figures derived from *Panorama of EC Industry 1993* (Brussels: Commission of the European Community, Eurostat, 1993), pp. 25–47.

7. See the interesting analysis of the history of the car industry in D. H. Ginsburgh and W. J. Abernathy, eds., *Government, Technology and the Future of the Automobile* (New York: McGraw-Hill, 1980).

8. Dennis L. Meadows, Danielle H. Meadows, et al., *The Limits to Growth*, A Report to the Club of Rome's Project on the Predicament of Mankind (New York: A Potomac Associates Book, Universe Books, 1972).

9. To mention but a few, Barry Commoner, *The Closing Circle* (New York: Bantam Books, 1971); J. K. Galbraith, *The Affluent Society* (Boston: Houghton-Mifflin, 1958); H. Brown, *The Challenge of Man's Future* (New York: Viking Press, 1954); René Dumont, *Chine surpeuplée, tiers-monde affamé* (Paris: Le Seuil, 1965); Robert Jungk, *Tomorrow Is Already Here* (New York: Simon and Schuster, 1954).

10. World Commission on Environment and Development, *Our Common Future* (Oxford: Oxford University Press, 1987).

11. The principle of responsibility has been analyzed and developed by Hans Jonas, *Das Prinzip Verantwortung. Versuch einer Ethik für die Technologische Zivilization* (Frankfurt: Insel, 1985).

12. An interesting reading on this subject is Ugo Lucio Businaro, *Globalization. From Challenge Perception to Science and Technology Policy*, FAST, Commission of the European Communities, Brussels, December 1992.

13. See Joseph A. Camilieri and Jim Falk, *The End of Sovereignty? The Politics of a Shrinking and Fragmenting World* (Alderslot, UK: E. Elgar Publishers, 1992).

14. See Michael Walzer, "Between Nation and World," *The Economist*, September 11, 1990, pp. 51–54, and Jean Chesnaux, "Les ONG: ferment d'une société civile mondiale, *Transversales*, no. 24, Paris, 1993.

15. Jean Chesnaux, "Après Rio: tout reste à faire," *Transversales*, no. 16, Paris, 1992.

16. See *The Earth Summit's Agenda for Change*. An easily readable version of Agenda 21 and the other Rio Agreements, Centre for Our Common Future, Geneva, 1993.

17. Stephan Schmidheiny with the Business Council for Sustainable Development, *Changing Course—A Global Business Perspective on Development and the Environment* (Cambridge, MA: MIT Press, 1992).

18. A first attempt to distinguish the three phenomena was made by Michel Beaud. See also Riccardo Petrella, "La mondialisation de l'économie, une hypothèse prospective" in *Futuribles*, Paris, September 1989.

19. George Modelski, *Principles of World Politics* (New York: Free Press, 1972).

20. Fernand Braudel, *Civilisation nationale, économie et capitalisme-XI$^e$–XVIII$^e$; 3 vols.* (Paris: Armand Colin, 1979).

21. A well-documented and in-depth analysis and discussion of globalization is contained in Winfried Ruigrok and Rob van Tulder's doctoral dissertation, *The Ideology of Interdependence*, University of Amsterdam, June 1993, 497 pages.

22. Ibid., p. 26. These authors consider that Ohmae's *ideology of globalization* has both a domestic and foreign target. Japanese people are advised to behave as "good world citizens" and to foster good relationships with the local communities where they chose to set up establishments. The term *glocalization*, invented by the Japanese, responds to such a need. The Japanese government is urged to reduce its role in the domestic economy (cf. our previous analysis on the process of weakening the welfare state) and to dismantle remaining trade and investment barriers to foreign companies, in conformity with GATT regulations. The message to Western business people and government representatives, in Ruigrok's and van Tulder's opinion, is to welcome rather than oppose Japanese internationalization.

23. See Jeffery Henderson and Manuel Castells, eds., *Global Restructuring and Territorial Development* (London: Sage Publications, 1987).

24. Jeremy Howell and Michaelle Wood, *The Globalization of Production and Technology* (London and New York: Belhaven Press, 1993).

25. Ruigrok and van Tulder, in *The Ideology of Interdependence,* mention a working paper of the Berkeley Roundtable on the International Economy (BRIE), *Globalization and Production,* University of California, Institute of International Status, Working Paper, 1991, which reports that in 1990 some 670 publications in prominent business and economic journals had "global" and "globalization" in their titles—up from only 50 in 1980.

26. Anthony G. McGrew, Paul Lewis, et al., *Globalization and the Nation-states* (Cambridge: Polity Press, 1992), p. 22. We are aware of the fact that this proposition is not shared by other people in research, politics, and business. Many people consider that the importance and novelty attributed to globalization is simply overstated. See, for instance, P. Patel and K. Pavitt, "Large Firms in the Production of the World's Technology: An Important Case of Non-globalization," *Journal of International Business Studies,* First Quarter, 1991, pp. 1–21. Generally speaking, they believe that the most significant track of contemporary societies remains the "national system." In this view, the *national system of innovation* is of far greater importance and plays a much more decisive role than all the global processes we have described. See in particular the thesis by Michel E. Porter, *The Competitive Advantage of Nations* (London: Macmillan, 1990).

27. According to the consecrated formula used by Daniel Bell (author of *The Coming of Post Industrial Societies*) in *Towards the Year 2000* (Boston: Houghton-Mifflin).

28. A strong criticism of the perverse effects associated with the maintenance of a multitude of nation-states defending their absolute sovereignty has been developed since the 1950s, by among others, Pugwash, the association of scientists created by Albert Einstein and Bertrand Russell after Hiroshima. See Joseph Joseph, President of Pugwash, "Removing Incentives to Waging War," *Pugwash Newsletter,* October 1991.

29. See Riccardo Petrella, "Technology and Firm," *Technology Analysis and Strategic Management* 1, no. 4, 1989.

30. See the rather ill-founded proposition of Henry Wendt in *Global Embrace: Corporate Challenge in Transnational World* (New York: Harper, 1993).

31. The thesis that the economy of a country is less and less dependent on national firms, technology, and capital is the central argument of Robert Reich in *The Work of Nations. Preparing Ourselves for Twenty-First Century Capitalism* (New York: Knopf, 1991). See also the theoretical and documentary-rich study by Michel Beaud, *L'Economie mondiale dans les années '80* (Paris: La Découverte, 1989).

32. The debate between the pros and cons regarding the shift from national to global capitalism has been enriched recently by the debate on "communitarian" (acceptable, good) and "wild" (rejectable, bad) capitalism. Lester Thurow and Robert Reich in the United States, for instance, are supporters of "communitarian" capitalism.

They are closer to the line of reasoning of most German leaders who believe in the *sozialmarket Kapitalismus*.

33.  The thesis in favor of the shift toward a postcapitalist society has been developed by Peter Drucker in *A Post-Capitalist Society*. The opposition between good and bad capitalism is defended by Michal Albert in *Capitalisme contre capitalisme* (Paris: Le Seuil, 1991).

34.  Charles Albert Michalet and Michel Beaud are among the strong supporters of this thesis. In Michalet's view, globalization is *the deregulation of national financial markets and the subsequent internationalization of capital flows*. In the early 1980s, as production investments were lagging in large parts of the industrialized world, a surplus of capital circulated on a national and a global scale, searching for short-term, lucrative investments. Hence, the 1980s became the period of "casino capitalism" in Susan Strange's definition *(Casino Capitalism* [Oxford: Blackwell, 1986] or the "raider era" in Michalet's terms) *Global Competitiveness and its Implications for Firms* [Paris: OECD, OSTI/SPRI 89.7, 1989]).

35.  See in particular Michael Aglietta, Anton Brender, and Virginia Coudery, *La globalisation financière: aventure oblige* (Paris: CEPII, Euronomica, 1990).

36.  All data flows are taken from Ugur Muldur, *Les formes et les indicateurs de la globalisation*, FAST, Research Document, Commission of the European Communities, June 1993.

37.  John Hagedoorn and Jan Schakenraad, *The Role of Interfirm Cooperation Agreements in the Globalization of Economy and Technology*, FAST, Commission of the European Communities, Brussels, November 1991.

38.  A state-of-the-art study concerning the growth of interfirm strategic alliances up to 1985 including a review of major studies available at that time is Francois Chesnais, *Technical Cooperation Agreements between Firms. Some Initial Data and Analysis* (Paris: OECD, 1986) and Riccardo Petrella, *Cooperations technologiques européennes* (Brussels: Dossier FAST, 1987).

39.  See Richard J. Barnet and J. Cavanagh, *Global Dreams: Imperial Corporations and the New World Order* (New York: Simon and Schuster, 1994).

40.  Cf. William H. Davidow and Michael Malone, "The Virtual Corporation," *Business Week*, February 8, 1993. This corporation has no similarity at all with the "virtual corporation" (*enterprise virtuelle*) described by Devi Etthoffer in *L'entreprise virtuelle ou les nouveaux modes de travail* (Paris: Editions Odile Jacob,1992) and based on new forms of organization of production made possible by the new information and communication technology.

41.  See the overview of foreign direct investment in the 1980s by United Nations Centre on Transnational Corporations (UNCTC), *World Investment Report 1991. The Triad in Foreign Direct Investment* (New York: United Nations, 1991), p. 82.

42.  Cf. Jacques Delcourt, *Les fondements des transferts sociaux dans une économie globale*, a report to the Euro-American Conference on "Globalization of industrial

Economy. A Challenge to the Social Contract," May 28–30, FAST, Commission of the European Communities, Brussels.

43. On destabilization see Pierre Jallade, *The Crisis of Distribution in European Welfare States*, Trentham Books, 1989, and on a broader comparative basis, A. Pfaller, I. Gough, and G. Therbirgh, *Welfare Statism and International Competition: The Lesson of Five Case Studies*, a report to the Conference mentioned in note 20. Concerning possible future evolutions, see Hugues de Jouvenel and Charles Charpy, *Protection sociale. Trois scénarios contrastés à l'horizon 2000* (Paris: Editions Futuribles, 1986).

44. *Bericht des Bundesregierung zur Zukunftsicherung Standortes Deutschland*, Bonn, September 1, 1993.

45. "Dutch efforts to mend social security net take lead in Europe," *Wall Street Journal Europe*, December 1, 1993.

46. Mario Albornoz et al., "America Latina: ajuste con equidad?" A report for the FAST program, University of Buenos Aires, July 1991.

47. As reported by Audrey Choi in *Wall Street Journal Europe*, September 17–18, 1993, p. 4.

48. OECD, *Employment Outlook—July 1994*, Paris, 1994.

49. Cf. *Employment Outlook—July 1992*, OECD, Paris, 1992, and *Employment in Europe*, Commission of the European Communities, Brussels, 1992.

50. See Pauline Conroy and Niamh Flanagan, *Women and Poverty in the European Community*, Commission of the European Union, Employment, Industrialization and Social Affairs, Brussels, 1993.

51. Cf. Roy Pahl, *Divisions of Labour* (Oxford: Blackwell, 1984).

52. The concept of "lean production," its characteristics, implications, and consequences, are analyzed in J. P. Womack, D. T. Jones, and D. Roos, *The Machine that Changed the World* (New York, Toronto, and Oxford: Rawson Associates, McMillan, 1990). A discussion of a possible alternative European specific model of production, called "Anthropocentric Production System" (APS) is found in Franz Lehner, *Anthropocentric Production Systems: The European Response to Advanced Manufacturing and Globalization* (Luxembourg: FAST, Publications Office of the European Communities, 1992). See also Peter Brodner, *The Shape of Future Technology, The Anthropocentric Alternative* (London: Springer, 1990). A comparative analysis of different production scenarios for advanced industry is found in Fritz Rauner and Karin Ruth, *The Prospects of APS. A World Comparison of Production Models* (Brussels: FAST, Commission of the European Communities, 1991).

53. See Amin Rajah, *Services. The Second Industrial Revolution* (London: Butterworth, 1987).

54. See the results of extensive research carried out by BIPE and INSEE in France for the Department of Labor on the potential of job creation of ten groups of "solidarity services," "Nouveaux emplois de services! Les 10 services de solidarité," *Futuribles*, Paris, no. 174, March 1993, pp. 5–26.

55. Regarding recent debates on the issue one may consult, in French, "Faut-il partager l'emploi? Vers une révolution du travail," *Le Monde Diplomatique*, Paris, March 1993, pp. 11–17, and the special volume edited by *Futuribles* on "Temps de travail. Réduction et aménagement du temps de travail dans les pays industrialisés, tendances et enjeux," nos. 165–166, May–June 1992, 252 pp. Among English titles see, in particular, D. Bosch, P. Dawkins, and F. Michon, *Working Time in Fourteen Industrialized Countries—An Overview* (Gelsenkirchen: Institut für Arbeit und Technik, 1992).

56. Cf. Christophe Freeman and Luc Soete, *Macro-Economic and Sectorial Analysis of Future Employment and Training* (Brussels: Commission of the European Communities, October 1991).

57. The alternative was developed among others by Samir Amin, *Le développement inégal* (Paris: Editions Minuit, 1973); and, by the same author, *La déconnexion. Pour sortir du système mondial* (Paris: La Découverte, 1986).

# Chapter 2

1. A reference to the two lines of directions is made in Bernard Preel, *L'Euroconsommateur dans l'archipel planétaire,* FAST, Commission of the European Communities, October 1991, pp. 4–18 and following.

2. Koichi Minaguchi (President of Nomura Research Institute in Japan), argues that because the market economy has spread throughout the world, "a new era is beginning in which countries both cooperate and compete on the basis of a market economy. In this process, we will be shaping a new world map." Opening speech to the 1993 Tokyo Forum (December 12, 1992), *Reshaping the World Economy Map, Toward Global Revitalization of the Market Economy*, Tokyo, Publications of the Club Foundation for Global Studies, Tokyo, 1993, pp. 13–14.

3. Zhang Zhangli and Yuam Enezhen, "The Development of Chinese Private Economy and its limitative," *Shangai Academy of Social Papers*, Shanghai, 1992. See also Ford S. Worthy, "When Capitalism Thrives in China," *Fortune*, March 9, 1992; Y. Y. Kueh, "Foreign Investment and Economic Change in China," *The China Quarterly*, September 1992; and Roland Lew, "Les Espoirs du Capitalisme en Chine," *Le Monde Diplomatique*, Paris, April 1993

4. See special reports on China, "Beijing Rising," *Newsweek*, February 18, 1993, and "The Pains of Growth," *Newsweek*, June 10, 1993

5. It is interesting to remember that Japan was the first country where the government elaborated and made public in 1972 a detailed plan for the transformation of the country from an industrial society into an "information society." See *Plan for Information Society. A National Goal Towards Year 2000*, Japan Computer Usage Development Institute, Tokyo, 1972.

6. An interesting description, from a Japanese viewpoint, of how the Japanese are trying to manage the learning process of the new role in the context of South Asia and Southeast Asia development is offered by the Institute for Economic Planning for

Peace (Tokyo), *Economic Development and Regional Integration in Asian Regions. Current Status Analysis and Scenarios for Regional Cooperation*, A Report for the FAST Program, Commission of the European Communities, Brussels, May 1992.

7.  Japan Centre for Economic Research, *The Coming Multipolar Economy. The World and Japan in 2010*, Tokyo, May 1992.

8.  See the Economic Planning Agency, Government of Japan, *Report by the Year 2010 Committee*, Planning Bureau, Tokyo, 1991, and Japan Economic Research Institute, *Towards a New Global Design*, Tokyo, 1992; Network Institute for Research Advancement, *Japan. Towards the 21st Century*, Tokyo, 1981.

9.  Regarding the loss of technological leadership, see William Eaton, "US Losing its Edge in 10 of 11 High-Tech Fields," *Los Angeles Times*, November 18, 1992.

10.  Daniel Latouche, *The New Continentalism. Prospects for Regional Integration in North America*. A Report to FAST, Commission of the European Communities, Brussels, January 1992.

11.  Ibid.

12.  See section "Une société qui souffre et qui doute" of *Etats-Unis. Fin de Siècle*, Manière de voir no. 16, edited by *Le Monde Diplomatique*, Paris, October 1992, pp. 58–79.

13.  There are many other aspects of the European "problématique," and future prospects are discussed in Europrospective II, *Toward a New Social and Economic Development in Europe*, Presses Universitaires de Namur, Belgium, 1993.

14.  On recent evolution and prospects for the Arab world, see Charles Rizk, *Les Arabes ou l'Histoire à contresens* (Paris: Albin Michel, 1992), and Jean-François Nodinot, *Vingt-et-un Etats pour une Nation Arabe?* (Paris: Maisonneuve et La Rose, 1992).

15.  Alain Gresh, "Les Républiques d'Asie Centrale s'engagent sur des chemins divergents," *Le Monde Diplomatique*, Paris, December 1992.

16.  Cf. Max Jean Zins, "Le Modèle Indien balayé par le vent de l'Ouest," *Le Monde Diplomatique*, Paris, December 1992.

17.  An interesting analysis of Italy is presented by Robert D. Putnam, *Making Democracy Work, Civic Traditions in Modern Italy* (Princeton: Princeton University Press, 1993).

18.  An in-depth discussion of ongoing changes is offered by Pierre Lellouche, *Le Nouveau Monde. De l'Ordre de Yalta au Désordre des Nations* (Paris: Grasset, 1992).

19.  *The Social and Economic Impact of New Technology*, Society and Technology Towards the Future, 2 vols., FAST, Commission of the European Communities, Brussels, 1991.

20.  Cf. *Biotechnology Economic and Wider Impacts*, OECD, Paris, 1989; Albert Sasson and Vivien Costarin, *Biotechnologies in perspective*, UNESCO, Paris, 1991.

21. On these questions see STOA, *Bioethics in Europe*, Scientific and Technological Options Assessment, European Parliament, Luxembourg, 1992 and *Biotechnologia y sociedad, Percepcion y actitudes publicas*, MOPT, Madrid, 1992.

22. See, in particular, the conclusions from the case studies on "Risk Perception in Society and the Role of Public Information. The example of genetic engineering," in *Technology and Democracy*, 3rd European Congress of Technology Assessment, Copenhagen, November 4–7, 1992, edited by the Danish Board of Technology, 1993.

23. *Energy 2000*, Commission of the European Communities (Cambridge: Cambridge University Press, 1986), and *Energy in Europe. A View to the Future*, Commission of the European Communities, Luxembourg, 1992.

24. J. Goldenberg, J. B. Johansson, A. K. M. Reddy, R. H. William, and F. Rosenstiehl, *Energy for a Sustainable World* (Washington: World Resources Institute, 1987).

25. Bjorn-Andersen et al., *Information Society for Richer, for Poorer* (Amsterdam: North-Holland, 1982).

26. See "L'Ordinateur, l'homme et l'organisation," special issue of *Technologies de l'Information et Société* 3, nos. 2–3, Presses Universitaires du Québec, 1991; for a very useful discussion based on a paradigmatic case study on gender relations, cf. Inger V. Eriksson, Barbara Kitchenham, and Kea G. Tijdens, *Women, Work and Computerization* (Amsterdam: North-Holland, 1991).

27. Jim Northcott with Annette Walling, *The Impact of Microelectronics*, (London: Policy Studies Institute, 1988).

28. A very interesting analysis, focusing on the Japanese case, is contained in Martin Fransman, *Information Technology in Japan* (Cambridge: Cambridge University Press, 1990). See also Manuel Castells, *The Informational City, Information Technology, Economic Restructuring and the Urban-Regional Process* (Oxford: Blackwell, 1989), and Jorge Niosi, ed., *Technology and National Competitiveness* (Montreal: McGill University Press, 1991).

29. See Jacques Berleur et al., *Evaluation sociale des nouvelles technologies de l'information et de la communication*, Presses Universitaires de Namur, Belgium, 1990; Jacques Berleur and John Drumm, eds., *Information Technology Assessment*, IFIP (Amsterdam: North-Holland, 1991), and Riccardo Petrella, "Information and Communication Technology: Achievements and Prospects," in Jacques Berleur, C. Beardon, and Lauferr, eds., *Facing the Challenge of Risk and Vulnerability in an Information Society*, IFIP (Amsterdam: Elsevier, 1993).

30. Cf. Samuel P. Huntington, "The Clash of Civilizations?," in *Foreign Affairs*, vol. 72, no. 3, Summer 1993, pp. 22–49.

31. Ibid., p. 25.

32. Ibid., p. 29.

33. See Bernard Lewis, "The Roots of Muslim Rage," *Times*, June 15, 1992, pp. 24–28.

34. Huntington, "The Clash of Civilizations?" p. 39.

35. Kishore Mahbuban, "The West and the Rest," *The National Interest*, Summer 1992, pp. 3–13.

36. Ibid.

37. Benjamin R. Barber, "Djihad vs McWorld. Globalization, Tribalisms and Democracy," in *The Atlantic*, March 1992.

38. Philippe de Woot, with Xavier Desclee, *Le management stratégique des groupes industriels* (Paris: Economica, 1984).

39. On the new alliance, see Riccardo Petrella, "La mondialisation de l'economie: une hypothèse prospective," and Anthony G. McGrew, Paul Lewis, et al., *Globalization and the Nation-states* (Cambridge: Polity Press, 1992).

40. Philippe de Woot, *High Technology Europe—Strategic Issues for Global Competitiveness* (Oxford: Basil Blackwell, 1990).

41. See *Financial Times*, December 15, 1988.

42. The first to use the word "triad" was K. Ohmae in *Triad Power: The Coming Shape of Global Competition* (New York: Free Press, 1985).

43. UNCTC, *World Investment Report 1991*.

## Chapter 3

1. An extensive and interesting analysis of economic competition and related phenomena (market configurations, strategies of firms, role of the state, international dimension, etc.) is represented by M. Porter's books. See in particular Michael E. Porter, *Competitive Strategy* (New York: Free Press, 1980), and *The Competitive Advantage of Nations* (London: Macmillan, 1990).

2. This is the basic idea supporting the thesis of Ohmae, who first developed the concept of "Triad Power." See K. Ohmae, *Triad Power. The Coming Shape of Global Competition* (New York: Free Press, 1985).

3. Widespread concern over competitiveness arose around the end of the 1960s and beginning of the 1970s. The first report in the United States was the *Report of the President on U.S. Competitiveness* by the Office of Foreign Economic Research, U.S. Department of Labor, Washington, D.C., September 1980. One year later the *Report of Industrial Competition* was published by the European Management Forum, Geneva, 1981. Since then, this organization has become one of the most authoritative institutions in the field of the analysis of competitiveness. See note 10.

4. See Riccardo Petrella, "L'Evangile de la Compétitivité," *Le Monde Diplomatique*, Paris, September 1991.

5. See Lester C. Thurow, *Head to Head. The Coming Economic Battle among Japan, Europe and America* (New York: W. Morrow and Company, 1992); P. Kotler et al.,

*The New Competition. Meeting the Marketing Challenge from the Far East* (Englewood Cliffs, New Jersey: Prentice-Hall International, 1985).

6. *Le Monde*, June 8, 1993, p. 31.

7. Cf. *Winning in a World Economy*—University-Industry Interaction and Economic Renewal in Canada, Science Council of Canada, Report 39, Ottawa, April 1988.

8. From a lecture given by Kamar Singh, Program Manager, General Electric, at an international seminar organized by the Norwegian Academy of Technological Sciences in Trondheim, September 2–3, 1993.

9. An international scholarly based analysis of the various forms of competitiveness is contained in OECD, *Technology and the Economy*, Paris, 1992.

10. *The World Competitiveness Index* (WCI) is a yearly report compiled by the World Economic Forum in Geneva. The 1992 edition of the WCI includes thirty-six countries (twenty-four industrialized countries and twelve "developing" countries). It is calculated on the basis of eight groups of "competitiveness factors" with 300 criteria.

11. Second Report to the President and Congress, Competitiveness Policy Council, Washington, D.C., March 1993.

12. See *Beating the Crisis. A Charter for Europe's Industrial Future*. A report from the European Table of Industrialists, Brussels, 1993.

13. William Faff, "When Global Competition Means Regression at Home," *International Herald Tribune*, February 18, 1993, p. 4.

14. Ibid.

15. Quoted by Samuel Brittan, "Myth of European 'Competitiveness'," *Financial Times*, July 1, 1993.

16. Ibid.

17. Cf. Paul Krugman, "Competitiveness: A Dangerous Obsession," *Foreign Affairs* 73, no. 2 (March–April 1994): 28–44.

18. Ibid., p. 30.

19. Ulrich Hilpert and D. Hickie, *Archipelago Europe*, FAST, Bruxelles, 1991 and Emilio Fontela and Anders Hingel, "Scenarios on Economic and Social Cohesion in Europe," in *Futures*, March 1993, pp. 139–154.

## Chapter 4

1. Among the most interesting analyses supporting such a view, see Alexander King and Bertrand Schneider, *The First Global Revolution*, The Club of Rome (New York: Pantheon, 1991), and Lester Brown, Christopher Flavin, and Sandra Postel, *Saving the Planet* (New York: W.W. Norton, 1991).

2. Not everybody will agree with this proposition. Many share a more moderate assessment of the importance and long-term significance of the Rio Conference. A

strong minority even thinks that the conference was *another* megashow of international politics with no major effects on governments, industries, and people's behavior.

3. This is the perception that has been stimulating and guiding the debate, in some countries at least, concerning the way to implement the binding commitments specified in Agenda 21. Norway, Denmark, Sweden, and the Netherlands are among the countries where the debate has been extensive and significant as compared to the near-silence that has characterized the follow-up to the Rio Conference in all other countries of the world.

4. On the importance of mediation for the decisionmaking process in a context of growing globalization, see Ugo Businaro, *Globalization, From Challenge Perception to Science and Technology Policy*, FAST, Commission of the European Communities, Brussels, December 1992.

5. Cf. Marc Luyckx, *Les Religions face à la Science et à la Technologie, Eglises et Ethiques après Prométhée*, CEE, Brussels, November 1991.

6. All figures are taken from G. Ceragioli and L. Milone, *The Shelter Problem, Global Perspective 2010*, FAST, Brussels, May 1992. In the case of the homeless, some argue that the number of European and U.S. homeless is lower than the known estimates. See Christopher Jencks, *The Homeless* (Cambridge, MA: Harvard University Press, 1994).

7. See United Nations Centre for Human Settlements, *The Global Strategy for Shelter in the Year 2000*, Nairobi, 1990; and *World Habitat Day 1992. Shelter for Sustainable Development*, Nairobi, 1992.

8. Sean O'Siochru, *Global Sustainability, Telecommunications and Science and Technology Policies*, FAST, Brussels, January 1993.

9. For a balanced review and discussion of this problem, with a particular application to the relationship between the United States and Canada, see Centre Québécois des Relations Internationales, *Le développement culturel dans un contexte d'économie ouverte*, Quebec, April 1993.

10. Cf. Jaim De Mel and Arvind Panagariya, *The New Regionalism in Triad Policy* (New York: World Bank, 1992).

11. See *Globalization and Regionalization*, OECD Development Centre, Technical Papers, no. 61, April 1992, and Jason D. Lewis, "Southern Asia: Preparing for a New World Order," in *The Washington Quarterly*, Winter 1992, pp. 187–200.

12. Among the numerous examples that one may give of the contribution to the global approach by globalizing enlightened "oligarchies" is the well-known World Economic Forum in Davos (Switzerland), the Tokyo Global Forum, and the international Business Council for Sustainable Development. Regarding the Trilateral Commission, see J. S. Nye, K. Biedenkopf, and M. Shina, *Global Cooperation After the Cold War—A Reassessment of Trilateralism* (New York: Trilateral Commission, 1991).

13. The independent commissions created by the United Nations have produced some of the most enriching and debated writings on world problems—cf. the Brandt Report.

14. Earthscan Publications, London, 1992.

15. Ibid., p. 295.

16. Ibid., p. 301.

17. Cf. *Towards a New Global Design*, Japan Economic Research Institute, Tokyo, 1992. Another interesting Japanese contribution encompassing a broader spectrum is the report from the Japan Society for Technology, *A Proposal Concerning Technology and Human Welfare—Toward Building a Harmonious Global Society*, Tokyo,1992. The report is centered on three elements: Concept of Harmonizing Social Systems on a Global Scale; Basic Approach to the Creation of a Harmonious Social System; Basic Policy for Building for a Harmonious Global Society.

18. It is worth mentioning a few examples of work produced by members of this group. See Amin Amin, *Maldevelopment-Anatomy of a Global Failure* (London: Zed Books, 1990); Ed Mayo, *1992 European Wealth, Third World Poverty?* (London: World Development Movement, 1990); Duane Elgin, *Voluntary Simplicity: An Ecological Lifestyle that Promotes Personal and Social Renewal* (New York: Bantam Books, 1982); Brian Urquhart and Eskine Childers, *A World in Need of Leadership-Tomorrow's United Nations* (Uppsala: Dag Hammerskjöld Foundation, 1990); R. W. Cox, *Production, Power and World Order—Social Forces in the Making of History* (New York: Columbia University Press, 1987); R. Milibrand and L. Panitch, eds., *The Socialist Register 1992. The New World Order* (London: Merlin Press, 1992); S. Gill and D. Law, *The Global Political Economy, Perspectives, Problems and Policies* (Baltimore: Johns Hopkins University Press, 1988); James Robertson, *Future Wealth—A New Economy for the 21st Century* (London: Cassel, 1989); and the yearly reports 1990, 1991, and 1992 of Lester R. Brown et al., *State of the World* (New York: W. W. Norton and Co.).

19. See United Nations Development Program, *Human Development Report 1993*, New York, 1993.

20. These proposals are derived from Stuart Holland, *Towards a New Bretton Woods: Alternative for the Global Economy*, a FAST Report, Commission of the European Communities, FOP 325, Brussels, May 1993.

21. On this, see Saskia Sassen, *The Global City: New York, London, Tokyo* (New York: Princeton University Press, 1991).

# Index

ABACUS, 3
Advertising, xviii, 2–3, 104
Aerospatiale, 94
Afghanistan, 55
Africa, xiii–xiv, 2, 10, 13, 45, 47, 71, 73, 75, 78, 80, 92, 113
  regional integration in, 88, 118, 120
AFTA. *See* Asian Free Trade Area
Agenda 21, 12, 110, 130, 135–136
Aglietta, Michael, 24
Agriculture, 80
Aid, 26–27
Air transport, xiii, 3, 4, 5(table), 30
Albania, 47
Alcatel, 65
Algeria, 55
Alliances: strategic, 28–30
AMADEUS, 3
*America Can Do It*, 53
American Airlines, 3
Amnesty International, 10, 12
Anderson Consulting, 42
Apartheid: global, 80–83, 88
Arab countries, 55, 118
Argentina, 47
Asia, xiii, 10, 17, 28, 73, 75, 78, 113, 115. *See also* East Asia; South Asia; Southeast Asia; *various countries*
  development in, 45, 47
  and pax triadica, 84–85
Asian Free Trade Area (AFTA), 77, 87–88, 136

Asianization, 61
Association against Racism and Xenophobia, 10
Austria, 45
Autocracy, 90
Automation, 41
Automobile industry, xiii, 4, 6, 7(table), 27
  cooperation in, 28–30
Autonomy: regional, 55–56
Azerbaijan, 55

Barber, Benjamin R., 62
BASF, 65
Belgium, xii, 38, 56, 96, 131
Bell Atlantic, 30, 132
Berlitz-Belgium, 91
Bertelsman, 132
Beveridge, Lord, 35
Bilateralism, xvii, 100
Biodiversity, 135, 136
Bismarck, Otto von, 35
Booz-Allen & Hamilton, 97
BP, 65
Brandt Commission, 122
Braudel, Ferdinand, 15
Brazil, 10, 45, 46, 47
Bretton Woods, 13, 136
Brittan, Samuel, 98
Brundtland Commission and Report, 8, 14, 122
Bulgaria, 47

Bush administration, 96
Business, 136. *See also* Corporations;
    Multinational corporations
Business Council for Sustainable
    Development, 14
*Business Week* (magazine), 2

Cable News Network (CNN), 2
California, 54
Canada, 10, 12, 36, 56, 94, 129
Canary Islands, 45
Capital, xii, xiii, 149n34
    flows of, 23–27, 32
    and multinationalization, 16–17
Capitalism, xii, xviii–xix, 15, 44, 45,
    52, 148–149n32
    excesses of, xviii, 103, 104
    globalization of, 32, 112
    national, 23, 51
Caribbean countries, 26
Cars. *See* Automobile industry
Cayman Islands, 26
Central America, 46
Central Asia, 55, 88, 120
Central Economic Council (Belgium),
    xii, 96
Central Europe, 46, 54–55, 75, 80,
    113
*Changing Course*, 14
Chemical industry, 32
China, 2, 26, 35, 47, 55
    competition, 94, 98
    identity in, 51–52
    trade with, 45, 46
Cities, 80, 111, 140, 142
Citizens: global, 134
Citybank, 3
Climate change, 135, 136
Clinton, Bill, 53, 57, 96
CNN. *See* Cable News Network
Codevelopment, 120, 138–139
*Coming Back of America, The,* 53
Common good, 49–51, 86–87, 102
Communication systems, xiv, xv,
    113–114

international, 1–4
technology, 59–60
Commission of the European Union, 91
Community of Independent States, 87
Competitiveness, 89, 91, 105
    limits to, 97–105, 146n10
    promoting, 92–97
"Competitiveness: A Dangerous
    Obsession" (Krugman), 100–101
*Competitiveness of Europe and Its
    Enterprises, The,* 97
Competitiveness Policy Council (U.S.),
    xii, 96–97
*Competitive Strategy for America, A,*
    xii, 97
Complutenses University, 91
Computers, 3, 30
Construction, 30
Consumerism, 52
Cooperation, xvii–xviii, 51, 78, 98,
    126, 143–144
    of automobile industry, 28–30
    global, 107–108, 121
    in governance, 111–114
    knowledge and, 139–140
Corporations, 30. *See* Multinational
    corporations
    fair competitions and, 93–94
    state and, 64–70
Credit cards, 27
Croatia, 56
Culture, xiv, 22, 112, 114, 126
    and conflict, 61–62
    impoverishment of, 102–103
    tolerance of, 131–132
Cyprus, 45

Decisionmaking process, 112, 123
Decolonization, 46
Delinking, 49
    by countries and regions, 72–75, 80–83
Democracy, xi–xii, xiii–xiv, xvi, xviii,
    90, 102, 103, 145n2
    and global contract, 132–135
Denmark, 38, 59

Deregulation, 34, 36
Developing countries, 24, 40–41
Development, 10, 22, 122, 127
  limits to, 8–9
  paths to, 44–48
  sustainable, 130, 135–140

*Earth in the Balance: Forging a New Common Purpose* (Gore), 123
Earth Summit. *See* United Nations Conference on Environment and Development
East Asia, 47, 88, 115. *See also various countries*
Eastern Europe, xiii, 46, 54–55, 73, 75, 80, 113, 127
Economic Security Council (U.S.), 97
*Economie-monde*, 15
*Economist, The* (magazine), 2
Economy, xviii, 14, 36, 37, 38, 51, 80, 123
  globalization of, xi, xiii, 1, 18–21, 77, 90–91
  integrated world, 87–88
  liberalization of, 83–84
  multinationalization of, 16–17
  regionalization of, 77–78, 114–120
ECSC. *See* European Coal and Steel Community
Egypt, 45, 55
Elites, 13–14
Employment, 37, 42–43. *See also* Unemployment
ENEA. *See* Ente Nationale per le Energie Alternative
Energy, 129
Ente Nationale per le Energie Alternative (ENEA), 97
Enterprises: and states, 64–70. *See also* Corporations; Multinational corporations
Environment, xv, xvi, 8, 10, 122, 123
  protection of, xviii, 80, 104
  sustainable development and, 111, 135–140

Equal opportunity, 37
Ericsson, 65
Ethiopia, 56
Ethnic cleansing, 61
Ethnic groups, xv, 56, 61
Euroforum University, 91
Europe, 6, 17, 35, 78, 98, 115, 119. *See also* Central Europe; Eastern Europe; Western Europe; *various countries*
European Business Press Federation, 97
European Coal and Steel Community (ECSC), 115
European Community, 48, 54, 77, 85, 87, 115, 118–119, 127, 136, 137. *See also* European Union
  competitiveness and, 91, 97, 101
  identity and, 54–55
  trade and, 45–46
European Council of Competitiveness, 97, 145n4
European Monetary System, 54
European Union, 115, 125

FAO, 93, 122, 138
FDI. *See* Foreign direct investment
Finance, xiii, 19, 26, 38
*Financial Times* (newspaper), 2
Firms, 22–23, 28–29. *See also* Enterprises; Multinational corporations
First Report from ENEA on Italy's Competitivity in High-Tech Industries, 97
Ford, 28
Fordism, 79
Foreign direct investment (FDI), 31–32, 45, 71–72
*Fortune* (magazine), 2
"Four minidragons," 24, 102. *See also by country*
France, 10, 22, 28, 40, 54, 56, 59, 129
Friends of the Earth, 10
Fundamentalism: sectarian, 99

GALILEO, 3
Gallois, Louis, 94
General Agreement on Tariffs and
    Trade (GATT), 12, 33, 83, 87, 88,
    114, 137, 138, 147n22
    and market liberalization, 92, 93
General Electric, 95
Genetic engineering, 58–59
Genocide, 56
Germany, 22, 32, 37, 40, 54, 56, 59
    social welfare in, 35, 36, 38
Global Cooperation Commission,
    122–123
Globalization, xi, 1, 38, 63, 147n22
    of economy and society, 18–21
    of governance, 108–109
    impacts of, 121–125
    theory of, 15–16
GLOBECOM, 3
GM, 28
Gore, Al: *Earth in the Balance:*
    *Forging a New Common Purpose,*
    123
Governance, 17, 142. *See also* Social
    contracts
    cooperative, xvii-xviii, 108–109,
    111–114, 143–144
    and global contracts, 125–127,
    132–135
Great Britain. *See* United Kingdom
Great Maghreb, 78, 87, 136
Greenpeace, 10
Grotius, 15
G7, 86, 125
Gulf War, 6

Homelessness, 54, 113, 131, 156n6
Honda, 28
Hong Kong, 26, 52
Housing, 113, 127, 129
Human rights, 10
Hungary, 56
HydroQuébec, 129
IBM, 3, 65, 86
Identity

cultural and regional, 51–56, 112
    and insecurity, 56–57
IGU. *See* International Geographical
    Union
ILO, 122, 139
IMF. *See* International Monetary
    Fund
Immigration. *See* Migration
India, 2, 10, 47, 55, 61, 88
Indian Water Board, 129
Indonesia, 98
Industrial R&D Advisory Committee
    of the Commission of the European
    Union, 91
Industry, xii, xvii, 38, 68, 78, 80, 101,
    136
    alliances in, 28–30
Information and communication
    technologies (IT), 59–60
Information systems, xiv, xv, 59,
    151n5
    international, 1–4
Institute for Management
    Development, 96
Instituto Costaricano d'Electricidad, l',
    129
Integration: regional, 87–88
International Association for the
    Defense of Minority Languages,
    10
International Association of
    Cardiologists, 133
International Geographical Union
    (IGU), 122
*International Herald Tribune*
    (newspaper), 2
Internationalization, 15, 16, 28
International Monetary Fund (IMF),
    37, 45, 83, 88, 93, 136
    restructuring, 137, 138, 139
International Science Council Union
    (ISCU), 122
International Telecommunication
    Union (ITU), 3, 122
Internet, 4

Investment, 25, 34, 37, 68. *See also* Foreign direct investment
Iran, 55
Iraq, 55
ISCU. *See* International Science Council Union
Islamic movements, 55
Israel, 45, 110
IT. *See* Information and communication technologies
Italy, 10, 22, 28, 56, 97
ITU. *See* International Telecommunication Union
IWCIO, 122

Japan, xiii, xix, xx, xxi, 10, 16, 17, 22, 32, 35, 59, 61, 71, 143
automotive industry in, 6, 28
capital flows and, 24–25
competitiveness and, 94, 95, 96
governance by, 142–144
identity in, 52–53
information from, 2, 151n5
and pax triadica, 84–85
trade with, 45, 46
unemployment in, 40, 41, 79
Japan Economic Research Institute, 123–124
Jobs, 41–42, 43, 83, 97, 98
Jordan, 55
Justice: social, xviii, 38, 111

Khazakstan, 55
Knowledge: cooperative transfer of, 139–140
Kohl, Helmut, 94
Korea. *See* South Korea
Kriwet, H., 38
Krugman, Paul: "Competitiveness: A Dangerous Obsession," 100–101

Labor, xviii, xix, 17, 38, 41, 44
competitiveness and, 103, 104
delinking and, 81, 82

Latin America, xiii, 2, 10, 13, 32, 37, 71, 73, 92
development in, 45, 47
regional integration in, 115, 120
trade in, 46, 75
LDCs. *See* Less-developed countries
Leadership: technology, 57–58
Lebanon, 45
Leisure, 30
Less-developed countries (LDCs), 24
capital flows to, 25–27
Liberalization, 32, 33–34, 36
*Limits to Growth, The,* 8
Living standards, 97
Lomé Convention, 137, 139
Lyonnaise des Eaux, 129

Maastricht Treaty, 54, 85
McGrew, Anthony G., 19, 21
*Made in America: Regaining the Productive Edge,* 53
Maghreb. *See* Great Maghreb
Malaysia, 45
Manufacturing, 38, 60, 79
and trade, 73–75
Marginalization, xvi, xix, 53, 79
Market(s), 87, 92, 151n2
competitiveness and, 99, 100
deregulation and liberalization of, xix, 104, 149n34
globalization of, 19, 22–23, 27, 38
liberalization of, 32, 33–34
MCI, 30
Media, xiii, 30, 101, 125
Mercosur, 76, 77, 136
Mexico, 10, 12, 47
Middle class, 54, 56
Middle East, 47, 61, 75
Migration, xv, 15, 52, 80, 83
Military, 22
Minorities, 54, 55
*Missing Link,* 3
Mitsubishi, 65
Mitterand, François, 94
Modelski, George, 15

Modernization, 14, 23
Monsanto, 65
Multilingualism, 22
Multinational corporations, xiii, 63, 79, 102
   communications networks, 2, 3–4
   state and, 64–70
Multinationalization, 15, 28, 63–64, 132, 143
   of economy and society, 16–18
Muslims, 55, 61

NAFTA. See North American Free Trade Area
Nation-states, 21–22, 112
NATO, 85
Nestlé, 65
Netherlands, 10, 36, 37, 91, 96
Networks, 133, 134–135, 138–139, 140
New Deal, 35
Newly industrialized countries (NICs), 47, 71, 144
Newspapers, 2
Newsweek (magazine), 2
NGOs. See Nongovernmental organizations
NICs. See Newly industrialized countries
Nissan, 28, 68
Nixon, Richard, 23
Nonalignment, 45
Nongovernmental organizations (NGOs), xiv, 11, 13, 125
North America, xiii, xix, xx, xxi, 2, 13, 35, 45, 71, 84, 113, 143. See also various countries
   regional integration of, 88, 115
   trade in, 46, 75
North American Free Trade Area (NAFTA), 77, 87, 136, 137
Northern Telecom, 65
North-South issues, 10, 51, 93
Norway, 38
Nuclear energy, 59

Oceania, 115
OECD, 24, 38, 39–40, 41, 98
Ohmae, Kenneth, 15–16
Olivetti, 65
OPEC, 24
Organizations, 13. See also Nongovernmental organizations
Our Common Future, 8, 14

Pacific, 75
Pakistan, 55, 56
Palestine, 55
Palme Commission, 122
Panama, 26
Partnerships: global, 129–130
Pax triadica, 88
   impacts of, 84–86
Peru, 56
Planetary village, xiv, 3
PLO, 110
Poland, 45, 47
Politics, 118–119
Population, 78, 123
Poverty, 37, 46, 48, 51, 54, 127, 129
Power, xvii, 15, 22, 91, 100
Primo Rapporto dell'ENEA sulla Competitività dell'Italia nelle Industrie ad Alta Technologia, 97
Privatization, 34–35, 36, 37, 70
Production, xiii, 1, 44, 79
Productivity, xi, 42, 43
Products: life cycles of, 66–67
Protectionism, xvii, 100

Quayle, Dan, 96
Quebec, 56

Racism, 56
R&D. See Research and development
Red Cross, 10
Reengineering, 42
Regionalization, 109
   impacts of, 114–120
Reindustrialization, 80

Research and development (R&D), xii,
66, 67, 68, 101
globalization of, 19, 77, 78
Research and Technology Policy (EC),
91
Resources, xi, 89–90, 111
RETAIN, 3
Rio Conference. *See* United Nations
Conference on Environment and
Development
Roosevelt, Franklin D., 35
Ruigrok, Winifried, 15
Rumania, 47
Russia, 13, 35, 45, 47, 55, 75, 80

SABRE, 3
SADC, 136
S&T. *See* Science and technology
Saudi Arabia, 55
Scandinavia, 35, 36
Schmidheiny, Stephan, 14
Science and technology (S&T), 28
Science Council of Canada, 94
Scientific community, 125, 134–135
Security, 50, 51, 122
Self-interest, 50–51
Serbia, 56
Service sector, 4, 41–42, 79
Shelter, 113, 129, 130–131
Shipbuilding, 30
Siemens, 65, 86
Singapore, 26, 32, 94, 95
SITA. *See* Société International des
Telecommunications Aéronautique
Skerritt, John C., 42
Slovakia, 56
Small- and medium-size enterprises
(SMEs), 79
Smith, Adam: *The Wealth of Nations,* 32
Social contracts, 35
for basic needs, 127, 129–131
for cultural tolerance, 131–132
global, xix, 109–111, 124–126,
128(table), 132–135, 141
for sustainable development, 135–140

Social security, 35, 37, 51, 98
Société Générale, 65
Société International des
Telecommunications Aéronautique
(SITA), 3
Society, 38, 58
civil, 9–14, 142
globalization of, xi, xvi, 1, 18–21, 122
multinationalization of, 16–18
Society for Worldwide Interbank
Financial Telecommunications
(SWIFT), 3
South, 46–47, 48
South Africa, 45
South America, 113
South Asia, xiii, 37, 47, 71. *See also*
India
South Commission, 122
Southeast Asia, xiii, 2, 13, 46, 71, 84,
102, 143. *See also various countries*
regional integration in, 88, 115
unemployment in, 40–41, 79
South Korea, 26, 32, 45, 94, 95, 98
Sovereignty, 22, 112, 124, 148n28
Soviet Union, xiii, 55, 73, 113, 127
Spain, xiii, 56, 96
Spending: public, 36–37
Sri Lanka, 56
Sudan, 56
Sweden, 10, 13, 38, 56, 59
SWIFT. *See* Society for Worldwide
Interbank Financial
Telecommunications
Switzerland, 14, 38, 45
Syria, 55
SYSTEMONE, 3

Taiwan, 26, 45, 46, 52, 94, 95
Taxation, 68, 80
TCI, 132
Technology, xi, 38, 44, 66, 123
employment and, 42–43
global, xii, 19, 58–60, 77
innovations and wars, 83–84
leadership in, 57–58

Technonationalism, xvii, 100
Telecommunications, xiii, 2, 30, 60, 101
Telephones, 113
Texas, 54
Thailand, 26, 45
Third world, 48, 123
Thomson, 65
Thyssen AG, 38
Time (magazine), 2
Time Warner, 132
Tire industry, 68
"Towards a New Global Design," 123–124
Toyota, 28
Toyotism, 41, 79
Trade, xii, 15, 16, 25, 33, 64, 91
  and development, 136–137
  European Community, 45–46
  free, 12, 92–93
  in manufactured goods, 73–75
Trade unions, xiii, 142
Trade wars, 85–86
Transportation, 111. See also Air transport; Automobile industry
  infrastructures, 4–7
Triadization, 2, 49, 71–72
  factors in, 77–79
Tribalization, 62
Tulder, Rob van, 15
Tunisia, 45
Turkey, 26, 45, 55
Turkistan, 55
TYMNET, 3

Uganda, 56
UNCTAD, 122
Underdevelopment, 47
UNDP. See United Nations Development Program
Unemployment, xv, 56, 79–80
  as social issue, 39–44
UNEP, 122
UNESCO, 93, 122, 138
UNICEF, 138

UNIDO, 93, 122
United Arab Emirates, 45
United Kingdom, 10, 15, 22, 38, 40, 56, 96
  social welfare in, 35, 36
United Nations, 125
  global coooperation and, 122–123
  role of, 12–13, 88, 108–109, 133
United Nations Center on Transnational Corporations, 64
United Nations Conference on Environment and Development, 10, 11–12, 86, 110, 134, 135, 155–156n2
United Nations Conference on Population and Environment, 8
United Nations Development Program (UNDP), 122, 127, 132, 138
United Nations World Summit on Social Development, 144
United Provinces, 15. See also Netherlands
United States, xii, 6, 10, 11, 12, 15, 17, 22, 35, 36, 48, 52, 127, 142, 156n6
  capital flows and, 24, 25
  competitiveness and, 94, 96–97
  identity and, 53–54
  and pax triadica, 84, 85–86
  technology in, 42–43, 57, 58
  trade with, 45, 46
  unemployment in, 40, 79–80
  winning in, 94–95
Universal Charter of Human Rights, 11
Uruguay Round, 33
Uzbekistan, 55

Van Lennep, Emile, 98
Voluntary associations, 10–11
Volvo, 28

Wall Street Journal, 2
Water, 129, 130
WCI. See World Competitiveness Index
Wealth, 1, 12, 22–23, 44, 48, 87, 123

*Wealth of Nations, The* (Smith), 32
Welfare: social, xviii, xix, 104
Welfare state, 40
  dismantling, 35–38
Western Europe, xiii, xix, xx, xxi, 2, 13, 24, 32, 35, 36, 45, 71, 75, 79, 80, 88. *See also various countries*
  competition, 94, 95
  governance by, 142–144
  homelessness, 113, 156n6
  and pax triadica, 84, 85–86
  technology in, 42–43
WHO, 122
Woot, Philippe de, 63
World Bank, 37, 45, 83, 88, 93, 127, 136
  restructuring, 137, 138, 139
World Competitiveness Index (WCI), 96, 155n10
World Council of Churches, 133–134
World Economic Forum, 96
WORLDSPAN, 3
World Trade Organization (WTO), 136–137
World Wildlife Fund, 10
WTO. *See* World Trade Organization

Xenophobia, 56